NURSE
RESEARCH

Volume 6 Number 2 Winter 1998/99

Action research revisited

Issues in research

In the next issue of

NURSE RESEARCHER

Phenomenology

With authoritative articles on:
- *Philosophy and phenomenology*
- *Types of phenomenological approaches*
- *Critique of the Heideggerian approach*
- *Method slurring: the grounded theory/phenomenology example*
- *The misuse of phenomenology in nursing research*

Plus...
- *The 'Issues in Research' section, bringing you the big debates in nursing research*

Plus...
- *A comprehensive Research Round-up detailing conferences, lectures, current developments and whatever else is affecting nursing research.*

Nurse Researcher
Phenomenology
Out Spring 1999

See coupon at the end of the journal for subscription details.

Editorial

Nurse researchers in university departments should make their work more relevant to health service priorities. And if they are to maintain a strong position in the profession, they must create meaningful partnerships with practising nurses and trusts. These were the main messages in Professor Alison Tierney's inaugural lecture delivered to an audience of nurse researchers and academics at the University of Edinburgh last November. She told the audience: 'Nurse researchers must engage with the politically-set healthcare agenda. What is needed is more effective care based on evidence. To achieve this, academic researchers must become more responsive to the needs of clinically-based practitioners.'

She went on to emphasise the importance of multidisciplinary research and clinical partnerships in the political agenda. 'Multidisciplinary research is not a threat. It provides a new opportunity to address the invisibility of nursing's impact on the outcomes of patient care,' she said. She also told her audience that nursing research must 'widen its approach to examine the challenges the health service faces'. These challenges include, she said, the continuing move to primary care-centred service delivery, restructuring of acute hospitals, and the relentless and swift advance of technology.

University departments do have a significant role to play if progress is to be made, however. Progress will depend in part on nurse academics and researchers continuing to educate nurses in research techniques to increase nursing research's capacity. University nursing departments must also address their poor performance in successive research assessment exercises (RAE) although, Professor Tierney said, the RAE seems to 'favour already established successful disciplines'.

Clearly, these issues and the response to them are crucial to the future development of nursing research and nurse researchers. Implementing the findings of potentially influential research studies into daily clinical practice should be an integral part of the research cycle, accounted for at the early proposal stages of a project. Certainly there are issues around how to achieve this ideal, and much has been written in this journal, and many others, about the best methods for overcoming the barriers. But one of the starting points should, as Professor Tierney believes, be more overt and closer links between researchers and practitioners.

Perhaps this is an auspicious time to attempt this. Reconfiguration of trusts and the development of primary care initiatives, such as primary care groups, health improvement programmes and local health co-operatives, perhaps offer nurses the opportunity to increase their presence at influential commissioning levels. Developing links between these nurses and researchers could be beneficial to both groups, with nurses being able to arm themselves with up-to-date research findings – comprehensible, because they have been involved in the research process – and researchers gaining links to enable them to have direct impact on practice.

Notable examples of such collaboration already exist, but these are only the first steps. First and foremost, clinicians and researchers must show willingness to talk in a mutually comprehensible language, both to demystify the research process for many clinicians and to demonstrate greater respect for the role researchers play even if it is not considered to be 'hands on' practice. Only when both groups can communicate effectively with each other will progress become a reality.

Steven Black
Editor

Action research revisited

Changing practice through action research

Sarah Wallis BSc(Hons), DipN(Lond), RGN, ONC is Senior Lecturer at Middlesex Univeristy.

Action research offers researchers and practitioners a way of bridging divisions between them, argues Sarah Wallis.

Since the Briggs report of 1972 (1), the debate over whether nursing is a research-based profession has continued. In the interim, ideas about what exactly constitutes research have changed, evolved and developed in health care as well as in society in general. Action research is one approach that has developed in nursing over the past decade and appears to be growing in popularity with nurse researchers, who see it as a way of bridging the theory-practice gap. Action research can go beyond the confines of positivist or scientific paradigms and has the potential to generate and test action theories, thereby developing and emancipating practitioners. Exactly why nurses should use action research approaches and how they might utilise them to change practice within their own clinical areas is the focus of this paper.

Why nurses need to use research?
Research-based nursing practice is a professional requirement of every qualified nurse and is quite rightly expected by patients and

Action research revisited

their families. However, it has been identified that many nurses continue to practise in the way that they have always practised or rely on directions from senior ward staff or medical colleagues (2). Local custom and tradition are much more likely to dictate care practices than research (3).

Scientific knowledge and its application to practice has had very little influence upon the nursing practical reality (4, 5). Traditionally, nurses have not valued the wealth of theory that can support and develop much of their practice.

It seems that generating research data is not enough to influence practice. Practitioners lack the knowledge, skills and attitudes to integrate research into their care and to recognise and explore research issues in local areas of practice. These factors, combined with the criticism frequently made, that researchers continue to present their data and findings in ways that are not accessible to practising nurses (2, 6), are reasons why the utilisation of research findings in practice has been limited. Consequently, research findings have remained exclusively the domain of a minority in nursing who have the knowledge and skills to make sense of them. Because of this their effective utilisation has only occurred in isolated pockets of practice (6, 7). The issue of encouraging the nursing majority to integrate research into their practice is an urgent one if nurses are to continue evolving professionally and to maintain the trust of clients, patients and their families.

Research must be used and generated by the majority of nurses to fulfil both professional, personal and society's expectations of nursing both today and in the future. It seems that a change in attitudes is required by the majority of nurses practising today. The ethos of 'getting the work done', without a thought to its quality has to change to 'how can I get the work done in the most beneficial way?' Consequently, an awareness of the care choices available that are research based is essential, to be able to implement effectively research-based care in clinical areas. However, the application of research into practice is fraught with difficulties often related to the nurses' lack of understanding about research or the over-dependence on positivist approaches to generating knowledge (6) that have kept research at a distance from practice.

Although positivism has traditionally been the dominant philosophical research methodology, not only for nurses and other healthcare workers, but also in wider society, other approaches to generating knowledge are now acknowledged (8). Intrapersonal approaches that consider the nature of experiences of self and others have been expanded to interpersonal, incorporating social and critical theory (9). These evolving and diverse ways of generating knowledge have extended how and what knowledge is valued. Clinical practice research and approaches that incorporate change as part of their research approach can now be recognised (5, 10). It seems that the distance between what is researched and what is practised can be minimised by the adoption of alternative research approaches that can motivate practitioners to utilise their findings in practice within their methodology.

Why should nurses use action research?

If research is to have a significant impact on practice, researchers must incorporate aspects that consider problems unique to a local practice area. These need to be researched and the evidence generated used to change care accordingly. They also need to include the ability to monitor the effectiveness of care choices in research projects. Evidence-based practice has been defined as a process that can actively solve clinical problems (11). Steps that facilitate evidence-based practice have been identified by Rosenberg and Donald (12) (Box 1), and perhaps offer a way of using and developing research in practice areas. From this it can be appreciated that to utilise established research findings in care settings requires some considerable knowledge and skill from the practitioner. Nurses need to be facilitated to acquire these elements and integrate them into their role, if research-based care is ever going to be the norm rather than the exception. Action research approaches that require

Action research revisited

Box 1. Steps that facilitate evidence-based practice (Rosenberg and Donald 1995).

- Formulate a clear clinical question from the patient's problem.
- Search the literature for relevant articles.
- Evaluate (critically appraise) the evidence for its validity and usefulness.
- Implement useful findings in practice.

---

nurses to collaborate together to provide evidence-based care (13, 14), are strategies that can utilise effectively research in practice where perhaps other more traditional approaches have failed.

Action research is an approach that has gained increasing recognition from nurses. Its value is recognised through its ability to bridge the gap between theory, research and practice, bringing them into a closer alliance (15). Its main focus is very similar to the process involved in developing evidence-based practice (12), in that a local situation is examined, and problems are solved or effects of a change are monitored and evaluated (13, 16). The cyclical, dynamic nature of the action research approach combined with its collaborative philosophy, suggests that research can evolve and change according to participants' and researchers' needs (13, 17). Collaboration requires equity between team members: power and authority is shared. Participants offer their expertise which is positively acknowledged by all involved (18). In research terms this can ensure that a researcher's expertise is shared within the group and practitioners' experiential, intuitive knowledge is acknowledged. In this way, a sharing of ideas, expertise and knowledge helps to ensure that the research is rigorous, but remains grounded within practitioners' local reality.

The collaborative nature of this research approach is a real alternative to more traditional, hierarchical approaches to research and its utilisation. Its ability to include rather than exclude participants, its emphasis on active involvement rather than passive acceptance, seem to distinguish action research approaches from any other. The characteristics of this approach may offer us a way of successfully integrating research into nursing practice that nurses have not had before. It seems that practitioners can truly aim to 'gain the kind of knowledge that will help them to improve their practice, to gain a deeper understanding of the nature of nursing and have the ultimate objective of improving the quality of patient care' (3).

How do action research approaches influence nursing practice?
An example of the use of this action research approach in practice may serve to illuminate the unique characteristics of collaboration, personal development and change that have been identified in the literature and were evident within my most recent research study (19-21). In the project I studied the change from established care practices on one ward that advocated straight lifting of patients routinely after prosthetic hip surgery. These practices were in direct opposition to those recommended in the literature (22) and rolling patients after surgery was to be introduced. The implications of this change in practice were to be evaluated as the current literature was circumspect in regard to positive outcomes for patients and staff if correct care practices were adopted.

The action research approach was utilised to encourage research-based care and to generate new knowledge about the outcomes of this new care practice for staff and patients. This approach extended the process described by Rosenberg and Donald (12), in that it seemed both to apply deductively theory to practice and inductively monitor the effects of this on staff and patients to provide more theory about this phenomena. Using an action research approach moved away from the perspective that views knowledge as an external reality, to one in which it is viewed as context specific and situational (2), with theory and practice forming mutually constitutive elements in a dynamic relationship (23).

It seems that although action research approaches incorporate

Action research revisited

elements of applying established evidence to local practice areas and to monitor the results of this change, the whole action research cycle is much more than this. Indeed, in my study we not only applied research findings to practice, changed our practice and evaluated and monitored this process, but we were also able to generate data that extended the known theory on the outcomes, benefits or consequences of that change in practice. The development of theory relevant to local practice which then informs future care seems to be the element within action research that differentiates it from evidence-based practice and audit and confirms it as a valid, alternative research approach (15, 24).

The focus on collaboration and participation in the action research process is essential to its ability to facilitate change and education of participants. Titchen and Binnie (25) identified these qualities as important prerequisites to commencing any action research study. Hart and Bond (26) agreed, suggesting that educating and preparing the participants within the study is an integral part of the action research process. Nolan and Grant (24) suggested that in order for any change to be successful, including changes facilitated through an action research approach, a number of requirements must be met (Box 2). Obtaining as complete a picture of the study context and participants as possible is the crucial first step in the process of change and is essential to the effective progress of the action research project.

Although there are different ways of facilitating change in individuals (19), a normative re-educative approach was preferred in my study. Frequent individual and group discussions and debates were held initially to consider the issues detailed in Box 2. As the study progressed we returned to many of these issues again and also incorporated a more educational focus to any meetings between participants. The staff needed not only to be informed of research and the importance of accurate data collection, but also acquire a range of new clinical skills. Just telling the staff what to do would

---

Box 2. Requirements for effective change.

● There is a shared and explicit set of values acting as a guide for practice
● There is recognition that a problem area exists
● There is a common understanding of the problem
● There is a perceived need for change
● The situation is seen as amenable to change
● There is a focus on involvement and team building

---

not be enough to facilitate this change in practice. To be effective researchers and safe practitioners in their newly acquired skills, the nursing staff needed to understand what they were doing and be committed to its value for practice.

The full implication of these factors on my study had not been appreciated. They are the aspects of action research approaches that can be immensely time consuming (13, 27). I had begun to prepare the staff for the project about six to eight months prior to its official beginning and, as Meyer (27) has suggested, high levels of staff mobility meant that new staff constantly had to be prepared and involved in the study. As time elapsed it was difficult for me as the change agent and researcher to maintain my own morale and interest and I nearly gave up and adopted a more traditional approach to my research. The feelings that I had are quite interesting to note, because in the health service many action research projects may be affected negatively in this way, particularly if the researcher is working to a time-scale allotted normally to more traditional approaches. Indeed, studies may be shelved because of the protracted preparation time. The preparation of participants may be limited or rushed. A top down or autocratic approach to the process, that might in the short term be quicker, is likely to be favoured. Collaboration and participation that are central to the action research process could easily be compromised.

The nature of participation in action research projects can evolve

Action research revisited

and develop as the relationship between the researcher and
participants changes. It is central to the effective use of the action
research and its unique ability to facilitate a long-term change in
practice. Carr and Kemmis (28) recognised this in their identification
of three types of action research approaches. These are:
- Technical
- Practical
- Emancipatory, whereby the researcher becomes more and more
  involved with the participants.

These types are cited frequently in contemporary literature (26, 28,
29). Although Carr and Kemmis (28) suggested that only
emancipatory action research is true action research, Zuber-Skerritt
(30) recognised the value of all three; how studies are developmental
and can progress from the technical, through practical, to emancipatory
action research. Zuber-Skerritt's observations (30) were confirmed in
my study as I noticed that my role changed as did the participants', to
one based on equity and mutuality as the study progressed.

If I considered my research study in relation to the different types of
action research or, as Hart and Bond (14) referred to them, a typology
(discussed in Joy Lyon's article in this issue), my study was
predominantly technical or experimental in that it comprised a
comparative survey. During this stage of the study I needed to be quite
directive. I was teaching and educating the participants in research, the
study design, and the importance of utilising research in practice. The
structure of the study was mainly directed by me as the other participants
lacked sufficient confidence and specialist knowledge needed to design a
research study. Elements of the practical and organisational factors in the
typology were also present as the study progressed and my role became
much less directive. The more motivated participants became involved in
teaching the new clinical skills required to facilitate the necessary change
in practice and all staff were involved in data collection. At this point we
became more cohesive as a team and began to collaborate effectively.
Emancipatory, empowering elements to the study seemed to evolve or

become more noticeable towards its end.

Changing practice by using an action research approach seemed to necessitate the use of all three types of approach. My role as researcher/change agent seem to change subtly as the study evolved and the participants gained more knowledge and confidence. Normative re-educative strategies to bring about change were essential to facilitate collaboration amongst the team, but this did not exclude me from taking a directive role in the initial stages of the project. Although emancipatory elements were minimal and only noticeable at the end of the study, subsequently they have benefited the staff.

Conclusion

The involvement of the staff with the action research project and the collaborative development of the team seemed to uncover many qualities within the individuals that were further developed independently after the project had finished. All participants who were involved with the study now quite naturally question their practice and implement research findings more readily into their practice. Their increased knowledge and confidence seems to have enabled and empowered them to think critically about their practice and develop their role further. It seemed that the action research study had 'got the ball rolling' in terms of research, its utilisation and application and ability to change practice, but the momentum once gained continued long after the project had been completed. Indeed, perhaps what we had achieved was an ability for endless future learning, for new ways of thinking, speaking and acting that have already been identified by Gadamer, as cited by Waterman *et al* (17). This is perhaps one of the most important characteristics of action research approaches in terms of its potential to promote long-term change in the behaviour of clinical practitioners.

This is an element of action research that is recognised in the literature, but is often ignored by many action researchers (5, 27). Action research is reflexive in that it changes practice as a direct result of the research (5). The ongoing, independent activities of the

Action research revisited

participants in my study, long after its completion, suggest that they had gained an awareness of their ability to shape and mould their nursing practice. 'Reflection in action' seems to be stimulated within participants of action research projects (5, 27, 28). Reflection in action has a critical function as it reshapes what is being done at the same time as it is being done. Nurses can begin to use theories to influence decisions made while practising (31). Action research seems to go beyond monitoring or evaluating a change in practice because it also stimulates a change in the practitioners involved, who become more reflexive and are consequently able to initiate changes in their subsequent practice and hopefully share that expertise with other practitioners.

Action research approaches appear to offer a way of not only extending our knowledge about clinical practice problems, but also facilitating changes in practising nurses. Participants within the research project can gain knowledge and confidence about research and its utilisation. They can feel empowered and enabled to evaluate critically patient care and staff performance to provide effectively a high quality of care in their area of practice. The link between what is researched and practised is minimised as all qualified practitioners appreciate the relevance of research findings for their patients care and have the knowledge, skills and confidence to change and monitor their practice accordingly.

References.

1. Department of Health and Social Security. Report of the Committee on Nursing. *The Briggs Report.* London, HMSO. 1972.

2. Hunt M. The process of translating research findings into nursing practice. *Journal of Advanced Nursing.* 1987. 12, 101-110.

3.Walsh M, Ford P. *Nursing Rituals, Research and Rational Action.* Second edition. London, Heinemann. 1992.

4. Greenwood J. Nursing research: a position paper. *Journal of Advanced Nursing.* 1984. 9, 77-82.

5. Rolfe G. Going to extremes: action research, grounded practice and the theory/practice gap in nursing. *Journal of Advanced Nursing.* 1996. 24, 1315-1320.

6. Rolfe G. The theory-practice gap in nursing: from research based practice to practitioner based research. *Journal of Advanced Nursing.* 1996. 28, 3, 672-679.

7. Hicks C. A study of nurses' attitudes towards research: a factor analytic approach. *Journal of Advanced Nursing.* 1996. 23, 373-379.

8. Marks-Maran D, Rose P. *Reconstructing Nursing: Beyond the Art and the Science.* London, Ballière Tindall. 1997.

9. Holmes CA. Alternatives to natural science foundations for nursing. *International Journal of Nursing Studies.* 1990. 27, 3, 187-196.

10. Stevens PE, Hall JM. Applying critical theories to nursing in communities. *Public Health Nursing.* 1992. 9, 1, 2-9.

11. White S. Evidence-based practice and nursing: the new panacea? *British Journal of Nursing.* 1997. 6, 3, 175-178.

12. Rosenberg W, Donald A. Evidence-based medicine: an approach to clinical problem solving. *British Medical Journal.* 1995. 310, 1122-1126.

13. Gibbings S. Informed action. *Nursing Times.* 1993. 89, 46, 28-31.

14. Hart E, Bond M. *Action Research for Health and Social Care. A Guide to Practice.* Buckingham, Open University Press. 1995.

15. Holter I, Schwartz-Barcott D. Action research: what is it? How has it been used and how can it be used in nursing? *Journal of Advanced Nursing.* 1993. 18, 298-304.

16. Clifford C, Gough S. *Nursing Research: A skills based Introduction.* London, Prentice Hall. 1990.

17. Waterman H *et al.* Parallels and contradictions in the theory and practice of action research and nursing. *Journal of Advanced Nursing.* 1995. 22, 779-784.

18. Henneman EA *et al.* Collaboration: a concept analysis. *Journal of Advanced Nursing.* 1995. 2l, 1, 103-109.

19. Elliot J. *Action Research for Educational Change.* Milton Keynes, Open University Press. 1991.

20. Hendry C, Farley AH. The nurse teacher as action researcher. *Journal of Advanced Nursing.* 1996. 16, 193-198.

21. Hart E. Action research as a professionalising strategy: issues and dilemmas. *Journal of Advanced Nursing.* 1996. 23, 3, 454-461.

22. Love C. Rolling or lifting following hip replacement? *Professional Nurse.* 1994. 4, 456-464.

23. Carr W. Action research: 10 years on. *Curriculum Studies.* 1989. 21, 1, 85-90.

24. Nolan M, Grant G. Action research and quality of care: a mechanism for agreeing basic values as a precursor to change. *Journal of Advanced Nursing.* 1993. 18, 305-311.

25. Titchen A, Binnie A. *Changing Practice Through Action Research.* Oxford, National Institute for Nursing. 1993.

26. Meyer JE. New paradigm research in practice: the trials and tribulations of action research. *Journal of Advanced Nursing.* 1993. 18, 7, 1066-1072.

27. Carr W, Kemmis S. *Becoming Critical: Education, Knowledge and Action Research.* Basingstoke, Falmer Press. 1986.

28. Hart E, Bond M. Developing action research in nursing. *Nurse Researcher.* 1995. 2, 3, 4-13.

29. Simmons S. From paradigm to method in interpretative action research. *Journal of Advanced Nursing.* 1995. 21, 837-844.

30. Zuber-Skerritt O. *Action Research in Higher Education.* London, Kogan Page. 1992.

31. Jarvis P. Reflective practice and nursing. *Nurse Education Today.* 1992. 12, 3, 174-181.

Action research revisited

Starting out with action research

Kevin Hope MA(Gerontology), BSc(Hons), RGN, RMN, CertEd, RNT,
is a lecturer in nursing, School of Nursing, Midwifery and Health Visiting,
University of Manchester.

*Kevin Hope advises that before embarking on an action research
study, be aware of the effects the process may have on all participants,
not least the fact that the destination is not entirely certain.*

In this paper, I attempt to explore the considerations, dynamics and tensions
that might usefully be contemplated prior to engaging in action research, a
task which on the face of it, appears to be a straightforward one. However,
in consolidating my thoughts in this area it soon became apparent that this
was not necessarily the case.

The parallels that can be drawn between the process of action research
itself and its instigation have struck me very forcibly. Both are characterised
by decision trails and logistics which are context bound, complex and open
to confusion. In contrast, I feel that the literature, with notable exceptions,
tends to understate this complexity.

Everything is not necessarily neat and linear and this generates a problem
in attempting to describe the process of initiation. While I also may be
guilty of understating the complexity of the process, what follows is some
attempt to highlight the murkiness.

To provide some structure, the analogy of a journey will be used. I
believe this analogy is a useful one as an orienting framework and is helpful

in considering the options available.

Which direction?

There is clear agreement that any action research involves change in some measure (1-3), which in my analogy can be considered as a move from point A to B. Herein lies the first point of possible contention – why should we be aiming to go to point B? Why is change in this direction desirable or warranted? McNiff *et al* (4) argued that action research has an explicit value base and as a consequence one would expect an articulation of the rationale for change which may arise from different perspectives. McNiff *et al* (4) tended to focus on how an individual might do this, but it is also possible that such values or motivational forces can arise from a group who share similar feelings or have a certain disposition to their work. In addition, nurses operate in a professional context within guidelines and parameters laid down by professional bodies. Rules, regulations, guidelines and codes of practice can themselves serve as orienting or motivational forces which point us in the right direction, or which can serve as supportive evidence for defending the route being taken. The point is that we need to be clear about the purpose of and motivation behind the change.

There is, however, an important distinction to be made here between the journey that is valuable and the one that might be good, but only one person wants to go on. The distinction here is between making someone travel and persuading them to travel. This is a difficult issue because it relates to the impetus to bring about change which often requires a driving force and which is discussed later.

What route?

There are many ways in which one can set about a journey. We can be systematic and plan our journey down to the last detail. We buy a map, we know where we are and want to start from, we know where we are going and all we need to do is navigate a way from A to B by the most desirable route. The point about action research, though, is that it is a serendipitous journey. How can you plan ahead when you really only know the general direction, but not the route?

Kemmis and McTaggart (5) suggested that a reconnaissance phase is

Action research revisited

required. Such reconnaissance aligns with what Lewin (6) has described as 'fact finding'. Having identified one's thematic concern – the focus of change – then there is a need to take stock of the situation. Kemmis and McTaggart (5) suggested three areas to consider:

● Language and discourse
● Activities and practices
● Social relationships and organisation.

For each of these areas, history and contemporary practice, evidence of contestation and/or institutionalization can be considered. In effect they provide an analytical matrix within which to consider the current situation and the factors that have led it to the way it is now.

A very important aspect of such an approach is that it leads one to think of the nature of the data-set that helps you to establish the situation as it is now. If change is to be made then realistically you need to be able to show that change has occurred. However, if you do not know the future direction of the change then how do you know what to record or measure at point 1 (the start) to show that things are different at point x (the end)? Indeed, Waterman (7) argued that the validity of an action research project lies, to some extent, in the degree to which attempts are made to improve people's lives rather than practice itself and consideration to how such change can be identified is required.

One problem in this scenario relates to whether you have now actually started the action research process and to what extent one should involve others in this reconnaissance. Getting started on the journey and knowing that you have started are not clear-cut considerations.

Getting the journey started

The concept of motivational force mentioned above is important, but from where does the impetus to engage in an action research project derive? Robinson (8) approached this from the perspective of nurses working together to 'contest their subjugated position' in the hierarchy. He considered the main focus of action research to be an emancipatory one and in doing so, built the argument that the catalyst, one that overcomes nurses natural resistance to change, needs to be forced upon nurses by a realisation of their own 'pain and crisis'.

The language is forceful and dramatic, but captures an important aspect. While not necessarily aligning with his crisis perspective, believing that nurses are characterised by their ability to be proactive in their behaviour, I do recognise the importance of some form of cognitive dissonance (9) as a precursor to change, a sense of discomfort that something needs to be adjusted. The source of this can be wide and varied and the literature contains a multitude of examples of initiating forces.

The point is that an area needs to be 'ripe' for intervention and that participants are willing to engage and participate. Timing can make the difference and one could begin to question the point at which action research actually begins. My own experiences serve as an example. As leader to an elderly care module for undergraduate nurses I visited a local unit for old age psychiatry to organise placements. It was at this time I became aware of the presence of a multi-sensory room used for sensory stimulation for older people with dementia.

Coincidentally, I was pursuing further professional development in undertaking a research methods module that required of its participants the generation of a research proposal. The multi-sensory room fascinated me but even at this early stage an awareness of a sense of wanting to improve matters was evident. I offer the following quote from that proposal: 'Reflecting on my own clinical experience, a persistent sense of frustration is evoked in examining approaches utilised with regard to severely confused and demented clients. I realised these feelings were being reflected in research findings. It was with a sense of eager anticipation, then, that I came across the work of staff at a local hospital. In particular there was an ethos of enabling their clients and a sense of purpose. This was reflected in the homely environment and the utilisation of creative approaches to care.'

Subsequent to arranging student placements I had cause to visit the unit on several occasions and herein lay the genesis of an evolving and highly integrated relationship with staff on the unit. I was offered and took the opportunity to use the room in the clinical setting. Several other members of staff expressed an interest in being more systematic about its impact on

Action research revisited

patients and together we generated an assessment tool. However, it soon emerged that there were problems with using the room (10) and the original plans for an experimental study were shelved. The real issue was about why the room was not used. My colleagues and I decided it would be a good idea to be systematic in the way we went about this and consequently interviews were held with members of the multidisciplinary team to ascertain their views from which an action plan emerged.

The important point is that it took someone else to tell me that what I was doing was captured by the philosophy of action research and that my initial frustration with being unable to proceed with one form of research was now being supplanted by new energy derived from this paradigm. As Waterman *et al* (11) have argued, the problems of defining action research can be seen as a symbol of the potential for artistry and flexibility in the practice of nursing and action research.

Who are you travelling with?

There is the possibility that an individual can disguise their own agenda for change in the cloak of an action research project. How do you know that you are not that end of the continuum and avoid the criticism of pursuing individualistic and selfish goals or being guilty of 'evangelical verve'? Part of the answer lies in the extent to which democracy is evident. Action researchers do not generally travel alone. The concepts of collaboration and/or participation are ones with which many authors concur (1, 3, 12, 13), and are seen by many as a fundamental aspect which distinguishes action research from other forms of research. In an ideal world all group members would start at the same point in time and travel in harmony along the same route to reach the end of the journey. In the real world do not be surprised if this is not the case and some interesting dilemmas emerge.

It may be the case that others will only be persuaded to join you on your journey once you have started by yourself or with a colleague. The image becomes one of action research being the vehicle which derives its energy from a source which may begin as one or two individuals, but can grow as others join over a period of time. In my analogy, action research now

21

becomes a bus ride. But just like a bus people might want to stop and get off and one needs to think about the circumstances that promote a collective working together to the end point of the journey. What can be done to promote harmony?

Some authors have dealt with this problem by a process of initial screening. Meyer (14), for example, reported that it took her 62 interviews over a period of six months to identify a ward area where she felt the prospects of promoting lay participation in care might be maximised. Webb (15) spoke ward sisters about her plans and invited volunteers. This was moderated by her personal agenda of preferring to work in an area where her own clinical credibility would not be compromised. This point is also relevant to the desired goal of a harmonious journey and is captured by the debate as to where one needs to be located as an action researcher – inside or outside the research environment.

The fact that the usual aim of action research is to bring about some change in practice has meant that value has been attached to the action researcher having insights into the tacit knowledge and experiences of the practice area, that is, the practitioner as researcher (16). Conversely, there is the argument that nursing is in its infancy in terms of reflective practice (13), and that blind spots to vagaries of local custom and practice exist. An outside view, a fresh view, can highlight the previously hidden. Similarly, it could be argued that an individual nurse working in a particular arena is better placed to instigate and monitor action. However, questions have been raised as to how the hard-pressed clinical nurse finds the time and space to allocate to the process of action research (17). To this end some have argued that it is only through academic researchers working in professional development roles that action research can be successful (13).

A third option exists, an alliance model, and is one which appears to be growing in popularity. Here the (usually) academic researcher with access to resources and infrastructure supporting research, forms an alliance with an insider working in the clinical area with tacit working knowledge and experience. In this model the whole is seen as greater than the sum of its parts. Manley (18), in exploring the development of an advanced practitioner/consultant nurse post, highlighted the contextual prerequisite for the post-holder to have some form of organisational authority attached to

Action research revisited

their post and I believe that there are parallels in determining the success of an action research strategy. Although the 'insider' action researcher may not necessarily need to have such organisational authority, the question is raised as to whether having someone on board with such authority promotes success? Bellman (19) suggested that there was even the possibility that her co-researchers might face sanctions due to a perceived reprobate status, but that 'the ongoing support and *legitimate power* [my italics] of the nurse unit manager provided the catalyst for change and enlightenment'. This highlights the concept of permission.

Permission to travel

Problems relating to consideration of the 'route' are discussed above. This is especially problematic when explaining to others, particularly those who you need the support of to allow you permission to enter into and cross their domain. The classic approach to gaining permission is via the auspices of an ethics committee. While there is a variation in the nature and identity of such committees, I think it is fair to say that the notion of action research is not a framework that most committees deal with on a regular basis. Indeed, my own experience is that the necessary forms to be filled can often imply that a quantitative design is the norm and that a case for other approaches needs to be made. This is a situation that qualitative researchers are familiar with (20), but action researchers face an additional burden of not knowing the endpoint. The solution that seems most used is to describe the process as it is intended at the starting point, but that a rider needs to be included about the possibility, indeed the likelihood, of different directions emerging. To this end, an ethically sound piece of action research will bring to the attention of the ethics committee (in my own case through the directorate representative) changes in the direction and any ethical concerns arising. This leaves open the possibility of full ethical committee approval being sought again to take account of any major change of direction in the research design, for example, the action research moving from staff participation and views to patient participation and views.

Permission to travel needs to be sought at a wide range of levels and the concept of gatekeepers (21) is a relevant one to many forms of research. The informal links that need to be made and alliances that support the process must be thought through. It is in this area that action research can be seen to offer some ready-made solutions because of its democratic principles – the fact that one researches with rather than on practitioners means that, to some extent at least, potential gatekeepers are necessarily engaged in the process of research. In this respect one could argue that a successful action research project may be an index of the extent to which format and informal gatekeepers are engaged in the process, but this is idealistic. It is highly unlikely that all influencing bodies will come together to support one change process. It is the nature of human experience for there to be different opinions and values attached to a one-change project. So do not be too disappointed if you find at least passive resistance to change or some variation between rhetoric and reality: indeed, the exploration of such variation can be seen to be a fruitful line of inquiry in the research process itself.

What can be helpful, though, is some consideration as to how conflict resolution is to be managed. Some 'ground rules' within a collaborative group can be useful, but one is cautious of time being expended on dealing with 'what ifs' rather than actualities and there is a danger that the group and its focus on action can stagnate.

Resources needed for the journey

Time is a very important consideration in action research. As indicated, if change is an important part of the process then surely time must be allowed for such change to occur. In addition, time is needed for no change to occur because it would be morally contentious to push for change in the arena of the action research concern when there are other factors operating in the context impeding such a change (7). The action researcher needs to develop a sense of knowing when to push and when not to. Ideally the nature of the research will be open ended, but in reality there are limiting considerations. Increasingly, this takes the form of the research falling into the remit of an education programme, particularly for post-registration courses, which vary in length. While there is the allure of doing something to close the theory-practice gap,

Action research revisited

the possibility that this may not always be appropriate does not perhaps receive the same amount of consideration. There is a potential problem of trying to make the action research fit into a predetermined slot available for its completion which would not allow for the development of alternative action cycles.

Time is also required for the cycle of action research to occur. Fact-finding, analysis, action planning, implementation of the action plan and its subsequent evaluation are sequential considerations. Hyrskas (22) argued that action research should undergo a minimum of two cycles to be so categorised, although this appears to be an isolated view.

The group of co-researchers is an important resource and is prone to variation. Ideally it is constituted at the commencement of the programme and remains a constant feature. In the real world of clinical practice, however, due to staff turnover, inability to attend meetings, sickness, holidays and maternity leave this is seldom the case. Meyer (14), for example, reported 174 disruptions to the ward staff quota in a one year period. What can you do to limit the impact of or minimise such turnover? At one end of the spectrum replacement staff costs can be included in a funded study. At the other, be prepared fit into the timetable of the environment under study, to be receptive to the pressures that staff are under and for meetings not taking place. However, the notion of a 'virtual group' is also one that I believe will become more acceptable – one in which members are able to contribute to and influence the research by other means than formal meetings. In my own case this was promoted by the use of information technology, e-mail in particular.

Implied in the above, and something that needs to be made explicit, is that one of the most significant resources is you, the action researcher. Rolfe and Philips (23) identified four components of the personal qualities of an individual change agent which they consider highly influential. These are the:

- Personal
- Interpersonal
- Intellectual
- Educational.

To this end consideration needs to be given to the type of person you are and whether this form of research fits in with your own operational philosophy. I believe that, in fact, action research does align with many nurses' operational philosophy because, as has been pointed out, there are many parallels between action research and the process of nursing itself (11). In addition, I also believe that most nurses are equipped with the skills necessary to act as action researchers, having well-developed interpersonal skills, flexibility to respond to new situations, a degree of social entrepreneurialism, a willingness to listen to alternative views, and the ability to be reflective and reflexive. The problem is in recognising and valuing such attributes in ourselves.

Conclusion

I am reminded of the story of the man lost in the countryside who asks for directions from a local. The reply 'If I were you I wouldn't start from here', seems to me to encapsulate the experience of entering into and managing an action research project. There are things that can be done to assist the smooth passage, but one needs to remember that the essence of action research lies in its flexibility and response to local needs. I believe the analogy of the journey, in particular a serendipitous journey, is a valuable one in considering the dynamics and tensions associated with engaging in action research. It tunes us into the range of possibilities in setting up and establishing such a project. It is only by recognising that such possibilities exist that we are in a better position to respond appropriately to them.

> *There is nothing more difficult, more perilous to conduct or more uncertain in its success, than to take the lead in a new order of things. For the innovator has for enemies all those who have done well under the old system, and but lukewarm defenders in those who may do well under the new.*
> **Machiavelli**

Action research revisited

References

1. Hart E, Bond M. *Action Research for Health and Social Care*. Milton Keynes, Open University Press. 1995.

2. Greenwood J. Action research: a few details, a caution and something new. *Journal of Advanced Nursing*. 1994. 20, 13-18.

3. Holter IM, Schwartz-Barcott D. Action research: what is it? How has it been used and how can it be used in nursing? *Journal of Advanced Nursing*. 1993. 18, 298-304.

4. McNiff J *et al. You and your action research project*. New York NY, Routledge. 1996.

5. Kemmis S, McTaggart R (Eds). *The Action Research Planner*. Third edition. Victoria, Australia, Deakin University Press. 1988.

6. Lewin G (Ed). *Resolving Social Conflicts: Selected Papers on Group Dynamics by Kurt Lewin*. New York NY, Harper and Brothers. 1948.

7. Waterman H. Embracing ambiguities and valuing ourselves: issues of validity in action research. *Journal of Advanced Nursing*. 1998. 28, 101-105.

8. Robinson A. Transformative 'cultural shifts' in nursing: participatory action research and the 'project of possibility'. *Nursing Inquiry*. 1995. 2, 65-74.

9. Festinger L. *A Theory of Cognitive Dissonance*. Evanston IL, Row-Peterson. 1957.

10. Hope K. Using multi-sensory environments with older people with dementia. *Journal of Advanced Nursing*. 1997. 25, 780-785.

11. Waterman H *et al.* Parallels and contradictions in the theory and practice of action research and nursing. *Journal of Advanced Nursing*. 1995, 32, 779-784.

12. Carr W, Kemmis S. *Becoming Critical: Education, Knowledge and Action Research*. London, The Falmer Press. 1986.

13. Meyer J, Batehup L. Action Research in health care practice: nature, present concerns and future possibilities. *NT Research*. 1997. 2, 175-184.

14. Meyer JE. New paradigm research in practice: the trials and tribulations of action research. *Journal of Advanced Nursing*. 1993. 18, 1066-1072.

15. Webb C. Action research: philosophy, methods and personal experiences. *Journal of Advanced Nursing*. 1989. 14, 403-410.

16. Elliott J. *Action Research for Educational Change: Developing Teachers and Teaching*. Milton Keynes, Open University Press. 1991.

17. Waterman H. *Meaning of Visual Impairment: Developing Ophthalmic Nursing Care*. Manchester, Victoria, University of Manchester. 1994.

18. Manley K. A conceptual framework for advanced practice: an action research project operationalizing an advanced practitioner/consultant nurse role. *Journal of Clinical Nursing*. 1997. 6, 179-190.

19. Bellman L. Changing nursing practice through reflection on the Roper, Logan and Tierney model: the enhancement approach to action research. *Journal of Advanced Nursing*. 1996. 24, 129-138.

20. Merrell J, Williams A. Participant observation and informed consent: relationships and tactical decision-making in nursing research. *Nursing Ethics*. 1994. 1, 163-172.

21. Hammersley M. *What's wrong with Ethnography?* London, Routledge. 1992.

22. Hyrskas K. Can action research be applied in developing clinical teaching? *Journal of Advanced Nursing*. 1997. 25, 801-808.

23. Rolfe G, Philips LM. The development and evaluation of the role of an advanced nurse practitioner in dementia – an action research project. *International Journal of Nursing Studies*. 1997. 34, 119-127.

Action research revisited

Developing and evaluating an acute stroke care pathway through action research

Frazer Underwood RGN, DipHE Nursing, is Stroke Services Co-ordinator, and Jane Parker RGN, RMN, Dip Nursing, MA (Human Resource Management), is Process Manager (Neurology), Leicester Royal Infirmary NHS Trust.

Here the authors describe how action research was integral to changing practice when a care pathway was introduced for patients following a stroke.

While considering the challenges associated with effective multidisciplinary working, we examined alternatives to traditional practice and custom. Eventually this process led the stroke team at Leicester Royal Infirmary NHS Trust to develop a care pathway across the full spectrum of stroke services. This article presents the initial phase of the project from implementation to evaluation focusing on acute stroke management, detailing the events which prompted the care pathway approach and explaining why action research was used as a methodology for change.

Action research revisited

Background

Six hundred people each year are admitted to Leicester Royal Infirmary (LRI) following a stroke, 50 per cent of whom will be admitted to the Acute Stroke Unit (ASU). The ASU comprises a six-bedded bay area within a 20-bedded acute neurology ward. The unit is managed as an individual entity fully supported by a dedicated multidisciplinary team.

This project began in June 1997, following the relocation of the ASU from an integrated medical ward, where it had been founded four years previously, to its current position in the neurology ward. The process of re-establishing the unit within an altogether different setting prompted the professionals involved to question inherited practices. There is strong evidence to suggest that patients who receive organised inpatient stroke unit care have better clinical outcomes than those receiving conventional care management (1). However, since commencing in post the Stroke Services Co-ordinator had become aware that many acute stroke patients were not referred to the ASU and consequently, were exposed to considerable variations in care and management.

He believed that the reason appropriate stroke patients were not admitted to the ASU was that length of stay on the unit was too long and, therefore, effectively reduced the availability of beds for new acute admissions.

Snapshot of practice

Average length of stay for patients in the ASU was in fact 10.3 days, which compared less favourably with other acute stroke units around the country, where length of stay was on average seven days in the acute phase, this was also supported in the literature (2). Reason for this were unclear, but witnessed variations in care even within the ASU highlighted that we were not communicating while working. In order to obtain a more informed picture, the team's stroke research nurse undertook a review of all documented care stroke patients had received in the first seven days in the ASU for a two-month period. In addition, data for a similar period detailing the care that patients in the general medical directorate had received was collected for comparison.

Between September and October 1997 data was gathered for a sample of 32 patients who had been admitted through the ASU and a sample of 23 patients in the medical directorate. Comparison between these groups highlighted a disparity in care as suspected, but of particular interest were issues around variations in access to the multidisciplinary team.

Table 1 shows referral rates to the professional groups included in both samples within the first seven days of admission. It illustrates that patients managed in the ASU had had a greater percentage of referrals to the professional groups, with the exception of occupational therapy and social work services, which were limited at the time, than patients managed in the medical directorate.

Table 2 shows the response of the professional groups to complete initial patient assessment and demonstrates the generally favourable response to patients in the ASU.

Table 1. Percentage of patient referrals to the professional groups (Sept/Oct 1997).

	ASU (n=32)	MD (n=23)
Physiotherapy	78%	65%
Occupational therapy	22%	43%
Dietitian	47%	30%
SALT	59%	43%
Social work	9%	17%

Table 2. Percentage of patients assessed by therapists (Sept/Oct 1997).

	ASU (n=32)	MD (n=23)
Dietitian	47%	30%
SALT	59%	43%
Social work	9%	17%

Action research revisited

Access to documentation from all professional groups directly involved in patient care was found to be limited, as each profession kept patient information in different locations. In this instance we could not find the data we needed from the physiotherapy and occupational therapy groups.

The variations in care referred to earlier were clearly demonstrated in the data detailing swallowing and nutrition assessments. In the month preceding the review, the ASU had undertaken a comprehensive Initial Safe Swallowing Ability Checks' (ISSAC) training programme for all qualified nurses to allow them to assess stroke patients before they are allowed to drink and eat. This quality measure had been initiated in response to guidelines linked to improved outcome for stroke patients (3) and was obviously reflected in the results.

Sixty-six per cent of ASU patients had in fact had an ISSAC assessment on admission, compared to zero per cent in the medical directorate. It was interesting to note however that neither patient group had had a nutrition assessment, even though it is directorate policy, and considered best practice, to perform one on admission (3).

Why care pathways?
There is a considerable body of literature on care pathways dating back to the early 1970s. However, as a novice researcher and more of a practitioner than a theorist, the Stroke Services Co-ordinator was often confused by terminology and conflicting opinions towards the effectiveness of the care pathway approach. Nevertheless, during periods of wandering in the wilderness of research rhetoric he found an article which clarified the subject. The paper by Hotchkiss (4) explained the fundamentals of care pathways, and dispelled many of the myths which are commonly associated with the concept. In addition the paper concluded with practical pointers for success to assist newcomers in the art of pathway development.

Although much of the literature relating to the use of care pathways in acute stroke care identified clear benefits for the organisation, patients and associated clinical outcomes (1,5-9), little is offered by way of practical application. Thus it was a turning point in my review of the available literature to find such clear pointers for the application of care pathways. The next challenge was to find a suitable methodology for implementation.

Why action research?

The work of Gibbon and Little (10) proved a useful starting point for the novice action researcher. Their paper described how action research influenced and improved rehabilitative stroke care for patients by preparing nurses to participate fully in the interdisciplinary approach to stroke management. Drawing on the work of Nolan and Grant (11) they concluded by listing six critical success factors believed to contribute towards effective action research (11). This six point list represented perfectly the stroke team's position at that time (Box 1).

Box 1. Nolan and Grant's summarised requirements for action research.

- That there is a shared and explicit set of values acting as a guide for practice
- There is recognition that a problem area exists
- That there is a common understanding of the problem
- There is a perceived need for change
- That the situation is amenable to change
- That there is a focus on involvement and team building

Lauri's commentary (12) added to this as it referred to four elements of the action research formula that mirrored the nursing process. In Lauri's description of the cyclical characteristics of the methodology, the Stroke Services Co-ordinator identified similarities between action research and the steps involved in the audit and change management processes.

Action research revisited

Greenwood (13) is also a strong supporter of action research, claiming that it is the method most appropriate for nursing as a discipline. Greenwood has been particularly critical of the poor uptake of research by nurses which, she believes, has led to the concept of the theory-practice gap. She concluded by stating that, in short, action research attempts to effect change in the functioning of the real world. As a practitioner working in the very real world of an activity-driven NHS trust, this appealed to the Stroke Services Co-ordinator's personal philosophy.

Hunt's paper (14), reflecting further on practical techniques to close the theory-practice gap, supports Lewin's cyclical approach (15, 16) as an effective methodology. It is composed of three elements: fact finding, action and evaluation (17). This appealed to the team as a straightforward method reflecting customary practice which they could identify with. This model was chosen to develop and introduce the acute stroke care pathway.

Research design

The three processes identified by Lewin's conceptual framework (15,16) are summarised as:
- An educational phase or fact finding process where data is collected, the problems are clarified and ideas for a solution are discussed
- The 'action' part of the research process where objectives are set, plans developed and the pathway implemented
- The evaluation phase, created for feedback and to allow the acceptance or rejection of innovations.

Educational phase Members of the project team were elected to pursue the pathway's development and to communicate progress. Staff were selected for their commitment to the concept and a willingness to become key players. Included were representatives of all the therapy groups, that is, occupational therapy, physiotherapy, dietetics, speech and language therapy. The stroke outreach nurse, principal stroke pharmacist, stroke consultant and stroke services co-ordinator were also included.

His role became that of co-ordinator which allowed him to work on a one-to-one basis with each of the professional groups, and encourage each to focus on their specific responsibilities when assessing, planning care and giving treatments. He could also support individual group members to work and learn at a comfortable pace.

Each group examined their own profession's current practice through case-note review and feedback of findings to their colleagues. Information on existing service agreements was made available to allow for comparison with care actually delivered. In turn this was benchmarked against considered best practice. Finally, the literature was searched for guidelines and evidence to support best practice. An example of how this worked in reality can be illustrated by the following account relating to dysphagia management.

Nursing, speech and language therapy, and dietetics all make a significant contribution to dysphagia management in Leicestershire. These key players, who were employed by the community trust, along with the nurses, had raised concerns regarding documentation of dysphagia management, which they perceived to be cumbersome and repetitive.

Consequently a working party was formed the remit of which was to clarify the issues and develop a simple, workable solution. A number of meetings ensued during which it became apparent that the management of care following an initial swallow assessment was confusing. Poor documentation was a significant factor adding to professionals' frustration, but it soon became clear that this was not the only contributing factor.

As each professional group began to identify their contribution to the management of dysphagia, a clear pathway of care for the patient experiencing this particular difficulty began to emerge. Staff were able to develop ideas about the actions required following the initial swallow assessment to produce a protocol, which healthcare professionals could then use to guide practice. The actual paperwork was kept in what became our first example of collaborative

Action research revisited

documentation, allowing free access for all groups. It was interesting to note how this exercise pulled together the responsibilities of each professional role, and clarified lines of accountability.

Action phase The discussion period and information obtained during the educational phase helped the team to determine an appropriate length of stay for acute stroke management.

A seven-day length of stay would mean a reduction of three days. The objectives of a seven-day stay would include agreement for long-term nutrition needs to be met, and a final discharge destination for rehabilitation or continuing care. It was anticipated that all necessary referrals and assessments should be complete within the seven-day span to allow this.

The pathway itself also evolved out of discussions which took place in the educational phase as we sought solutions to the challenges of managing time and resources within a seven-day span.

As the pathway concept translated into a visible document, we sent a draft copy to our audit department who organised the information into a format that could be scanned which was then fed into a database. This allowed us to access performance standards and audit practice. To complement the pathway, we also began to work towards a whole package from collaborative assessment material to a patient and relative copy of the pathway.

Our work was constantly evaluated within the team, and a number of minor changes were made to documentation as our thinking matured and the concept of pathways became clearer.

Eventually we felt ready to share our work with the wider neurology team and set up a series of communication forums designed to explain what care pathways were, how they can promote evidence-based practice and how they work in the 'real' world. Eight one-hour sessions reached over 40 staff and interest was high. This led to further amendments as the wider audience prompted discussion around the timing and measurement of therapeutic interventions. The final version of the pathway was ready for launch in November 1997.

Evaluation phase The evaluation phase consisted of a two-part exercise combining staff perceptions to the change in practice and the influence of change on clinical outcome.

Staff survey Staff were surveyed two months post-implementation by questionnaire using both open and closed questions in addition to Likert-type inquiry. The response rate was 49 per cent and questions were asked under three headings: development, implementation and evaluation.

● *Development* Action research calls for constant feedback at every stage of the process. The questionnaires returned by those professionals involved in the care pathway's development showed that 83 per cent rated their involvement as good or very good. Nursing staff working in the ASU, however, felt differently; they felt much less included in the development stage, reflected by the following comment: 'The ASU nurses should be seen as experts in the care pathway" use, therefore they should receive better preparation to assist the rest of the team.'
   To me this suggested that ownership of the care pathway was limited to the implementation group and had not cascaded to other nurses.

● *Implementation* Seventy-five per cent of all respondents rated the preparation during the month before pathway implementation as good or very good. Most respondents agreed that workshops provided a firm knowledge base about the nature of care pathways and their value in practice.

● *Evaluation* The questionnaire allowed people to comment on personal perceptions of care pathways and/or practical experiences. Seventy-two per cent of respondents had had occasion to use the care pathway since its implementation: 30 per cent used the care pathway 'regularly' compared to 70 per cent responding 'seldom' or 'never'.

   There was a strong correlation between confidence in using the paperwork and 'regular' use. This was evident from the comment: 'Initially [the care pathway] appeared confusing, yet after I used it a couple of times it was relatively easy to use.'

Action research revisited

Several people expressed concern regarding the apparent increase in pathway paperwork and supporting documentation, but again there was a good correlation between perceived increase in paperwork and regular use. The more negative comments were directed at some of the wider organisational issues and were not always relevant. Others implied criticism of the documentation pack.

There was a mixed reaction to the perceived influence of care pathways on relatives and patients, some staff commented that care pathways are 'not easy for relatives to understand'. This, however, contrasted with comments such as 'patients and relatives seem better informed and ask less about care'.

We are planning a formal relative and patient evaluation of care pathways in the near future.

Positive aspects of the care pathway related to the manner in which it focused the stroke team towards a consistent and structured approach. The care pathway had also, it was suggested, contributed to the involvement of team members who had previously considered themselves to be on the boundary of the stroke team. A further characteristic and one of critical importance to the Stroke Services Co-ordinator was the widely expressed opinion that standards of care had been enhanced by the care pathway, and that individual accountability had been clarified.

Clinical outcomes

This element compared data relating to clinical outcomes pre-implementation, to that six months post-introduction.

The most notable improvement was in average length of stay, which had been reduced by three days, from 10.3 days to 7.3 days. It was not surprising to find that activity during that period had increased by 38 per cent.

Specific data on the care pathway also identified improvements in performance against national guidelines. An example worth noting relates to swallow assessments. We now check safe swallow on 86 per cent of patients within 24 hours of admission which represents a 20 per cent improvement since the introduction of the care pathway. Alternatively we could also see why 14 per cent of patients had not been checked within 24 hours of admission, and take this information back to the team.

Other data relating to nursing activity have shown that a nutritional screen on admission to the unit had improved from none prior to care pathway implementation to 75 per cent when evaluated. And the nurse-led aspirin administration protocol, where a registered nurse gives aspirin on confirmation of an ischeamic stroke, improved by 25 per cent.

Conclusions

Findings from our evaluation indicated a positive influence on outcomes of care and the main benefits can be summarised as:

● Improved quality of care through team agreement of optimal timing of care and treatments
● Reduced variations in care as everyone works to the same, agreed action plan
● Improved patient satisfaction following on from a pre-planned programme of management which includes the patient as well as the family
● Multidisciplinary clinical audit brought to the bedside
● Reductions in the amount of paperwork through collaborative documentation
● A strengthening of the multidisciplinary team; the pathway's development process helped identify professional roles and responsibilities and improved team member's understanding of each others' contribution
● Reduced length of stay through implementing a co-ordinated approach to assessment, investigations and therapeutic interventions during inpatient stay
● Stroke patients can be assured of an evidenced-based approach to the care they receive.

The key mechanism for the success of the project was undoubtedly the use of action research and the contribution of that method to addressing the theory-practice gap.

Action research revisited

References
1. Stroke Unit Trialists' Collaboration. Organised inpatient care (stroke unit) care after stroke (Cochrane Review). The Cochrane Library. Issue 3. Oxford, Updated Software. 1998.
2. Odderson IR, McKenna BS. A model for management of patients with stroke during the acute phase. *Stroke*. 24, 12, 18-27.
3. Gordon M *et al. A National Clinical Guideline Recommended For Use in Scotland by the Scottish Intercollegiate Guidelines Network (SIGN). III: Identification and Management of Dysphagia*. Edinburgh, SIGN. 1997.
4. Hotchkiss R. Integrated care pathways. *NT Research*. 1997. 2, 1, 30-36.
5. Moody L. Different strokes. *Health Service Journal*. 1996. 106, 5502, 26-27.
6. Falconer JA *et al.* The critical path method in stroke rehabilitation: lessons from an experiment in cost containment and outcome improvement. *Quality Review Bulletin*. 1993. 19, 1, 8-16.
7. Hydo B. Designing an effective clinical pathway for stroke. *American Journal of Nursing*. 1995. 95, 3, 44-51.
8. New T. On the right path. *Health Service Journal*. 1995. 105, 5473, 28.

9. Romito D. A critical path for CVA patients. *Rehabilitation Nursing*. 1990.15, 3, 153-155.
10. Gibbon B, Little V. Improving stroke care through action research. *Journal of Clinical Nursing*. 1995. 4, 93-100.
11. Nolan M, Grant G. Action research and quality of care: a mechanism for agreeing basic values as a precursor to change. *Journal of Advanced Nursing*. 1993. 18, 301-311.
12. Lauri S. Development of the nursing process through action research. *Journal of Advanced Nursing*. 1982. 7, 301-307.
13. Greenwood J. Nursing research: a position paper. *Journal of Advanced Nursing*. 1984. 9, 77-82.
14. Hunt M. The process of translating research findings into nursing practice. *Journal of Advanced Nursing*. 1987. 12, 102-140.
15. Lewin K. Action research and minority problems. *Journal of Social Issues*. 1946. 2, 34-46.
16. Lewin K. Frontiers in group dynamics: social planning and action research. *Human Relations*. 1947. 1, 143-153.
17. Ketterer RF *et al. The Action Research Paradigm. Evaluation and Research in the Social Environment*. New York NY, Academic Press. 1980.

Action research revisited

Applying Hart and Bond's typology: implementing clinical supervision in an acute setting

Joy Lyon RN, BNSc, PGDip Ed, MSc, is a teaching fellow, University of Southampton School of Nursing and Midwifery.

Hart and Bond's typology offers action researchers the opportunity to change practice systematically and with rigour, according to Joy Lyon.

This article describes how Hart and Bond's action research typology (1) was used to clarify the process of implementing clinical supervision. The project's aims were to:

- Generate an appropriate process of clinical supervision
- Identify contextual factors which contributed to or inhibited the implementation of clinical supervision
- Identify structures necessary for the ongoing support of clinical supervision.

The clinical supervision group (co-researchers) were experienced nurses engaged in developing new nursing roles which were diverse and involved working outside conventional ward nursing teams.

Action research revisited

The seven criteria listed by Hart and Bond (1) are discussed here in relation to the four action research approaches they describe. Comments made by co-researchers during the research study are included throughout to demonstrate how the typology was interpreted.

Patton (2) said, about qualitative research, that 'the process is the product'. This phrase haunted me throughout the research project, and in my view epitomises action research. The process of completing the research project has resulted in ongoing cycles, generated and informed by members of the co-researcher group, and it is significant that I refer to 'the process' so frequently in this article.

Action research has been variously defined by authors as an experiment of the simplest kind, a change experiment for the purpose of measurement, fundamentally qualitative and appropriate for organisational settings, resulting in comments that action research is amorphous (1). Susman and Evered (3) suggested that contemporary action research developed through limitations apparent in positivist research approaches, which were considered inappropriate for the study of human organisations. However, action research has also been criticised as being limited: it is not 'real' research (4); sloppy research could be excused by labelling it action research (1).

Holter and Schwartz-Barcott (5) tried to clarify confusion surrounding the use of action research in nursing. The philosophical basis of the various approaches, they stated, is in the natural sciences, historical hermeneutics or critical sciences. Hart and Bond (1) took a similar approach; identifying four approaches with seven criteria as a way of identifying the underlying philosophy. They suggested this be used in a matrix (Table 1, pages 54-55). Hart and Bond do not intend the typology to be prescriptive, but to be used as a guide to distinguish between different types of action research, helping to make sense of what is going on. By using the typology I was able to challenge claims about limitations in action research, as well as being better able to provide meaning to the process.

Clinical supervision has been described in a Department of Health document (6) as: 'A formal process of professional support and learning which enables individual practitioners to develop knowledge and competence, assume responsibility for their own practice and enhance consumer protection and safety of care in complex clinical situations.' The recommendation by the Department of Health (6) that clinical supervision be explored and developed further stimulated interest in the concept in the unit where the research project took place. The clinical supervision meetings themselves generated an enormous quantity of data for analysis.

Action research

The typology provided by Hart and Bond (1) relates to the fundamental beliefs of action research identified by authors such as Carr and Kemmis (7), Greenwood (8), Newton (9), and Hart anmd Bond themeselves. Action research should (amongst other things) be context related and collaborative, change practice and generate theory. Project design should incorporate these beliefs, the reality being that complete integration may vary over time. Recognition and acknowledgment of the degree of integration can contribute to the rigour of the research process.

Contextual Action research is situational and concerned with identifying problems within a specific context, attempting to solve the problem contextually. Practitioners are encouraged to make clear any salient aspects of a 'problem' and to examine the relationships between them. This examination must incorporate an awareness of relevant contextual factors which are often ambiguous and uncertain. It is, therefore, necessary for nurses to be aware of their personal and professional philosophy and how this can influence the process (7).

The achievement of a goal may be insufficient if a situation embraces nursing values which compete with the values of other people involved. Different understanding of a situation by participants can result in disagreement regarding the process required to achieve the goal. If the difficulties of achieving the goal outweigh the benefits to be gained, it may not be considered worthwhile – this involves real/ideal decisions. The clinical significance is arrived at by

Action research revisited

judgement based on attention to the details of participants and their world.

Collaboration Action research is collaborative, with teams of researchers and practitioners working together on a project and team members taking part in implementing the change. This involvement can increase awareness of traditionally accepted assumptions regarding practice (8). Questioning the *status quo* can be empowering for practitioners who recognise the effect 'taken-for-granted' assumptions can have on decisions made by others. Challenges to others may generate strong negative reactions from more powerful groups due, in part, to perceptions of status and self-esteem (10). This raises questions regarding illusions of autonomy, as opposed to real autonomy, which can influence practitioners' decisions/actions regarding responsibility for quality of patient care, regardless of lack of influence over allocation of resources. The action research process requires that issues of power be explored. Involving practitioners in the research process can have a developmental and empowering effect.

Change in practice Action research continuously monitors modifications in the ongoing situation, the objective being improvement of practice. Evaluation is necessary in order that feedback can be incorporated into the developing process, which benefits the current process rather than only being of benefit in the future. Effective management of both positive and negative evaluations has to be achieved, and can make the process feel uncomfortable to the researcher if the research project has been planned using more traditional research approaches.

Theory generation Action research should contribute not only to practice, but also to theory which is accessible to others. Oiler Boyd (11) suggested that this approach can encourage the use of research in practice, the clinical differences in the quality of peoples' lives being more meaningful than statistical significance testing. One reason theorising occurs, according to Greenwood (8), is related to the decision making process required to generate action and so bring about the desired changes. Practical reasoning underpins action theories aiming to identify and manipulate the relevant contextual factors which connect intention and action, thereby providing the link between reflection and action.

Action research approaches

The cyclical process of action research (12) comprises:
● Diagnosing the problem
● Planning action
● Taking action
● Evaluating the results of action
● Identifying general findings.

The problem is then re-diagnosed in light of the information gained from the cycle.

As development occurs throughout subsequent cycles, a spiral of ongoing related cycles develops. This spiral is informed by developments within the setting, with the components of the setting (for example, people, protocols, attitudes and so forth) contributing to the ongoing action research cycles. This dialectic effect has the potential to make research relevant to people in the setting and, because they are involved in the research design, understood by them.

Hart and Bond's four action research approaches may be viewed as a similar spiral, with an action research project moving between the approaches depending on the nature of the problem and the people involved at a specific time:
● The experimental approach resembles the scientific 'cause and effect' research approach
● The organisational approach attempts to solve problems by change management strategies
● The professionalising approach is rooted in the practice and aspirations of new professions such as nursing and teaching and aims to develop research-based practice
● The empowering approach involves identifying and preventing oppressive attitudes towards vulnerable groups, and the generation of practice/person-centered theory.

Action research revisited

Hart and Bond's seven criteria
Discussion of the criteria here uses data from my research project to
identify which of the four action research approaches apply in each
case.

Educative base This criteria involves raising awareness in the group,
thereby enabling them to identify what it is they need to learn. What
the group identifies may not accord with the action researcher's
thinking.

This research project began in the experimental approach of action
research with the researcher proposing ideas, however, it moved
rapidly towards the professionalising type with co-researchers
requesting structured reflective sessions during which aspects of
practice were described for exploration and discussion. The
discussion enabled group members to analyse issues pertinent to their
new nursing roles.

Initially, the sessions were held as part of my academic studies
(experimental approach); the co-researchers requested that sessions
continue with adaptations in membership, ground rules, and content,
to meet needs as perceived by them (professionalising approach).

Box 1. Participants' comments relating to 'educative' base.

● 'It's difficult to know what else we might need; we might need
  things we don't know yet; don't know what clinical supervision
  is yet; don't know what we need to know'
● 'They may not have been aware of doing it wrong'
● 'No recognition of skills; stand in never does it fully or
  properly; in four hours I am expected to sort out all the
  problems'
● 'Too many words – do they all mean the same thing; doing
  something with reflection rather than just reflecting; I thought it
  was automatic'

Co-researchers recognised that they did not know what they needed to know (Box 1) this resulted in the process being determined by me (experimental) (13). 'Don't know what we need to know' also related to the implementation of new nursing roles. One co-researcher told how she recognised her new role was being manipulated by others, to achieve short-term organisation goals (organisational approach), while long-term goals (professionalising) were being compromised. In reality this was a difficult situation, with the fundamental cause left unexamined and alternative solutions unexplored. This example highlights issues related to moving into previously unknown realms of nursing, and how essential it is to remain aware of professional values throughout.

Co-researchers identified that the process can appear deceptively simple causing them to underestimate the knowledge and skills required to undertake effectively clinical supervision or new nursing roles. This appears to reflect Benner's work on novice/expert nurses (14). The desired result produced by the process is more than one definition depending on the context (empowering approach).

Individuals in groups This criteria is related to group interactions and factors which influence these. The clinical supervision process was suggested by me (experimental) to complete this study. However, co-researchers had complete autonomy regarding attendance, although the ground rules designed by them required a commitment to attend (professionalising).

The co-researcher group was initially selected by me (experimental), but this developed in subsequent cycles to being open/closed by negotiation (empowering). Access to the group is available every four to five months and membership has evolved. This process can accommodate the need for confidentiality and development of trust, while responding to ongoing developments in practice (Box 2).

Data in this criteria do not fit clearly Hart and Bond's definitions, however, are probably nearer the experimental approach in relation to clinical supervision despite being a work group (organisational) members of which had initially self-selected (empowering). Data indicated the need for support, and issues of needing to demonstrate

Action research revisited

Box 2. Participants' comments relating to 'individuals in groups'.

- 'Need to feel confident to expose yourself; that's why clinical supervision needs to be confidential; ground rules are necessary; we have to 'role-model' a process, non-hierarchical, non-blaming culture'
- 'Group discussion provides individual with ability to deal with situation on her own'
- 'Collusion – not doing well, but I won't push you because I'm not doing well either; maybe that's where a lot of us are – we need to be pushed a bit; I hadn't anybody I could say this is what I'm doing – what's going on'
- 'I had something different to other staff; I'm trying to enhance what goes on, it was different; complementing it, not competing with it; I felt I was complementary; you are as well as – not instead of; you are for them as well as family; an extension of the team; you become part of the team'
- 'I felt I had support of G grades; I think they feel threatened; they don't know where they are going'
- 'I have to negotiate closely with the G grade; she has to trust me; she is committed to making it work; powerful figure – if she says "you're going to do it", they do it; she has to help me make it work; if she is not around it doesn't happen'

---

confidence while feeling unsure, thus the need to be able to discuss events freely in a supportive but questioning environment. This required an atmosphere where it was acceptable to express doubts, and seek alternative solutions to unique practice problems.

These comments related mainly to new nursing roles, showing how developments are unlikely to replace existing structures, but evolve to complement and enhance them. This aspect may not be fully understood by colleagues who feel threatened or believe they are perceived as being unable to cope.

Nurses developing new roles are often experienced nurses, able to deal effectively with familiar nursing problems. In their new role they can still expect themselves to cope well, however, the issues with which they are dealing may have previously gone unrecognised or been dealt with by someone with a different background. The co-researchers remained within the ward management structure while practising in a new arena, associating with other healthcare groups. The new nursing role or clinical supervision can generate unforeseen problems, and so be seen as the cause of problems that had not previously existed.

Lack of managerial authority was identified as well as the importance of gaining acceptance from ward managers in order to carry out new nursing roles or clinical supervision effectively. These aspects appear to identify cause and effect relationships between managers and workers (experimental/organisational).

Empowering individuals through action research and clinical supervision may create conflict between co-researchers and other groups; Meyer (15) warned novice action researchers about this problem. Clinical supervision may also empower individuals and the potential for conflict with other groups regularly arose, demonstrated at a combined meeting to discuss implementing clinical supervision throughout the unit.

Problem focus Hart and Bond (1) proposed that the intention of the action research process is to create a situation in which the 'real' and 'ideal' come closer together. Whoever identifies the problem determines the type of action research used, although Hart and Bond suggested that the term 'problem' gives the wrong impression of the action research process. For example, in this study 'implementing clinical supervision' was 'the problem'. This was relevant to managers or the researcher (experimental) in this instance, because clinical supervision was relatively unknown to co-researchers at the start of the project. However, this rapidly progressed towards a professionalising approach as issues emerged through discussion. Initially co-researchers raised related aspects such as preceptorship, role modelling, orientation programmes, which are managerial and professional requirements

Action research revisited

(organisational). How these aspects may be made more effective moves this area into professionalising/empowering action research approaches. Co-researchers identified different measurements of effectiveness (professionalising/empowering), however, they did not have the authority to implement clinical supervision due to established hierarchies (organisational) (Box 3).

Box 3. Participants' comments relating to 'problem focus'.

- 'If we devise it we can be ahead of the game; it will hit us from the top and may not be meaningful; you know what you wanted but others didn't'
- '[It] has to be rooted in practice'
- 'First time I was thinking of what was the difficult bits without going through the whole – the whole was easier; easier using a patient than a policy; drug error comes out of scenario, not contrived, not making it up, its real from their practice'

These comments indicate the co-researchers' appreciation of the need to define the problem focus (empowering), however, because resources and new initiatives frequently depend on evidence of value, success will be defined by managerial interests (experimental). This area requires further consideration in relation to the contextual beliefs of action research, and the debate about the value of process or product (product over process).

Change intervention How the change is implemented determines the action research approach. The experimental approach is likened to Lewins' original ideas (16, 17) with the intervention being analogous to the independent variable, and the consequences to the dependent variables of experimental research designs. Increased awareness of change theories has resulted in different approaches to implementing change, with bottom-up processes being considered more successful and empowering to participants.

The problem was framed in terms of research aims (experimental), as this study was initially conceived by the action researcher from past experience and interest in exploring the potential limitations and benefits of clinical supervision. However, early recognition of managerial aims (organisational) became apparent with co-researchers eager to identify professional aspects and, early in the meetings, questioning the value of clinical supervision. They were also involved in planning the process (professionalising/empowering).

Clinical supervision alone may not solve problems, but can be a contributory factor by helping participants reframe issues (Box 4).

Box 4. Participants' comments relating to 'change intervention'.

- 'I realised that was the wrong way to go about it; need to get in early with new staff, get established while all else is changing, becomes part of the new norm; there have been so many changes; I've got to earn my place'
- 'There is one sister who will support me, senior support half way there; rivalry; so long as majority see it as beneficial'
- 'Implementing roles in clinical area takes six months honeymoon then up to 18 months rejection'

These comments relate to the process of change and whether outcomes (experimental) or understanding of the meanings (empowering), is the focus. Co-researchers were able to identify longer term understanding and the impact of new nursing roles and clinical supervision. Possibly due to overlap of these areas a great deal of discussion occurred relating to 'change process' with little real suggestion of practical implementation, however, occasionally realistic proposals were made and may be implemented and evaluated.

The problem of 'habitualization' (18) was evident here: one co-researcher responded to suggestions that while she knew something, she might not have seen it with the freshness and clarity necessary in caring for individuals; and the value of peer comments was also acknowledged. This demonstrated the value of effective reflection in

Action research revisited

identifying espoused theory and theory-in-use.

Also identified was the lack of broad awareness of the function of new nursing roles/clinical supervision, therefore, resulting in an inability to move beyond the experimental action research approach. **Improvement and involvement** This criteria highlights that participants may not agree about what is defined as an improvement. With the experimental and organisational action research approaches the outcome is tangible with definitions agreed between groups. The empowering approach considers negotiated outcomes and pluralist definitions emerge through acknowledgement of the different views of various groups. This is essential when the action research study involves individuals, and takes place in a particular setting.

In this study the improvement could be defined as the group meeting regularly for an agreed time (experimental), however, in the empowering action research approach this would be insufficient due to lack of negotiated outcomes with other more influential groups associated with the acute setting. This criteria of action research aims to improve practice for the benefit of those people receiving the service (Box 5).

Box 5. Participants' comments relating to 'improvement and involvement'.

● 'I don't know exactly what I'm trying to achieve'
● 'Have to get something meaningful in available time'

These comments provide examples of how this criteria remains within the experimental action research approach, as outcomes of new roles are controlled and definition of improvement is consensual. However, during discussion it emerged that one co-researcher was unhappy with development in her role, although she acknowledged the development had seemed a good idea when proposed. This event appeared to epitomise the situational complexities of practice which serve to obscure the ideals espoused in the clinical supervision sessions. All co-researchers empathised with how easy it was to act spontaneously only to recognise later that the real issues had not been addressed.

Conflict was evident between achieving demonstrable outcomes, therefore maintaining or generating financial/time resource, and the pluralist outcomes required by individuals in complex situations.

Cyclical process Action research is seen as a 'spiral of cycles' comprising different phases (1, 7, 12). Hart and Bond (1) suggested that although one phase may dominate, all are interrelated and may at times be indistinguishable. Evaluation is considered essential for progress to occur. Experimental action research identifies cause and effect processes and may be limited by time, while empowering action research is open ended. This project may be considered to be a first cycle within a spiral, with the time limit being the submission date for the dissertation (experimental), however, the actual process is ongoing and relates more to professionalising or empowering action research. Continuing evaluation demonstrates an open-ended, process-driven spiral (empowering) (Box 6).

Box 6. Participants' comments relating to 'cyclical process'.

- '[We] may need to add things later; depends on what we discover; need to evaluate; you would alter what you did next time'
- 'Everything you said about jobs coming to fruition – now its beginning to happen; familiarity with process and pulling out key issues'
- 'I saw the role as implementing change; an amount of change in culture is required'

These comments demonstrate recognition of the need to evaluate actions and consider how to develop through cycles of research, action and evaluation. This evaluation and reflection does not always occur, and reasons for this appear to include lack of time, which may be a real issue. Effective evaluation can encourage practitioners to consider

Action research revisited

alternative strategies thus avoiding frustration and demotivation.
Research relationship and degree of collaboration This criteria refers
to the nature and extent of collaboration between action researcher and
co-researchers. In this study the relationship could be described as
falling in the experimental action research approach. While co-
researchers participated in the sessions as equals (professionalising), I
could be seen as having greater expertise due to my increased
awareness of both the research process and clinical supervision
(experimental) (Box 7).

**Box 7. Participants' comments relating to 'research relationship
and degree of collaboration'.**

- 'I knew what we were going to talk about before we went in; I
  wouldn't walk in and take over; one incident I said to nurse "if
  you want to do this without me"'
- 'She [G grade] has to trust me; she is committed to making it
  work; powerful figure – if she says you're going to do it – they do
  it'
- 'We introduced primary nursing; it was actually the F grade, she
  proposed it, did all the ground work, set up study days, it took a
  year, she got G grades on board, it meant a reversal of roles, you
  had to step back from being in control'

These comments demonstrate that the level of influence in the
process determines the relationship between the researcher and
respondents. This initially fitted the experimental approach.

Discussion within each session indicated developing recognition of
short/long-term, managerial/nursing, real/ideal, practice/theory
relationships. The appreciation that this was not a 'right/wrong'
debate, but a different perspective causing tension and debate, was
demonstrated as sessions progressed (professionalising/empowering).
The way forward may be to develop an understanding between the

two aspects which are not exclusive, although they can appear this way. Recognition of commonalities generated discussion which accommodated short-term needs while remaining true to long-term ideals. This allows response to contextual aspects which are influenced by the rapidly changing NHS, while retaining a nursing philosophy to guide the process.

Conclusion

Hart and Bond's typology (1) can appear complex, requiring an appreciation of a wide range of theoretical concepts . My recognition and understanding of these concepts have developed since commencing academic nursing studies after two decades of clinical practice. This again highlights the tension in the relationship between theory and practice. My experience in relating this typology to an action research project is that the experimental/organisational approaches may be appropriate for short-term evaluations, or when 'best practice' is unknown, however, immediate action is necessary. Professionalising/empowering approaches are necessary to evaluate long-term consequences and to relate the wide range of factors which have an impact on clinical practice. These approaches require research participants to recognise the dialectic nature of practice events and research. This means viewing situations in a multi-dimensional frame in which single events have numerous 'knock-on' effects. Hart and Bond's typology provided this multi-dimentional framework in which a single event (clinical supervision) was viewed in relation to the complex practice situation. This approach encouraged rigour in operationalising concepts, acknowledging the reality of a particular setting, and the contribution of the people within that setting, a process which necessitated clear articulation of philosophical values throughout.

Table 1. Hart & Bond's Action Research Typology (1)

Consensus model of society — Rational social management → Conflict model of society — Structural change

AR type Distinguishing Criteria	Experimental	Organisational	Professionalising	Empowering
1. Educative base	Re-education	Re-education/training	Reflective practice	Consciousness-raising
	Enhancing social science/administrative control and social change towards consensus	Enhancing managerial control and organisational change towards consensus	Enhancing professional control and individual's ability to control work situation	Enhancing user-control and shifting balance of power; structural change towards pluralism
	Inferring relationship between behaviour and output; identifying causal factors in group dynamics	Overcoming resistance to change/restructuring balance of power between managers and workers	Empowering professional groups; advocacy on behalf of patients/clients	Empowering oppressed groups
2. Individuals in groups	Social scientific bias/researcher focused	Managerial bias/client focused	Practitioner focused	User/practitioner focused
	Closed group, controlled, selection made by researcher for purposes of measurement/ inferring relationship between cause and effect	Work groups and/or mixed groups of managers and workers	Professional(s) and/or (interdisciplinary) professional group/negotiated team boundaries	Fluid groupings, self selecting or natural boundary or open/closed negotiation
	Fixed membership	Selected membership	Shifting membership	Fluid membership
3. Problem focus	Problem emerges from the interaction of social science theory and social problems	Problem defined by most powerful group; some negotiation with workers	Problem defined by professional group; some negotiation with users	Emerging and negotiated definition of problem by less powrful group(s)

	Experimental	Organisational	Professionalising	Empowering
4. Change intervention	Problem relevant for social science/management interests	Problem relevant for social science/management interests	Problem emerges from professional practice/experience	Problem emerges from members' practice/experience
	Success defined in terms of social science	Success defined in sponsors	Contested, professionally determined definitions of success	Competing definitions of success accepted and expected
	Social science, experimental intervention to test theory	Top-down, directed change towards predetermined aims	Professionally led, predefined, process-led	Bottom-up, undetermined, process-led
	Problem to be solved in terms of research aims	Problem to be solved in terms of management aims	Problem to be resolved in the interests of research-based practice and professionalisation	Problem to be explored as part of process of change, developing an understanding of meanings of issues in terms of problem and solution
5. Improvement and involvement	Towards controlled outcome and consensual definition of improvement	Towards tangible outcome and consensual definition of improvement	Towards improvement in practice defined by professionals and on behalf of users	Towards negotiated outcomes and pluralist definitions of improvement: account taken of vested interests
6. Cyclical process	Research components dominant	Action and research components in tension; action dominated	Research and action components in tension; research dominated	Action components dominant
	Identifies causal processes that can be generalised	Identifies causal processes that are specific to problem context and/or can be generalised	Identifies causal processes that are specific to problem and/or can be generalised	Change course of events; recognition of multiple influences upon change
	Time limited, task focused	Discrete cycle, rationalist, sequential	Spiral of cycles, opportunistic, dynamic	Open-ended, process driven
7. Research relationship, degree of collaboration	Experimenter/respondents	Consultant/researcher, respondent/participants	Practitioner or researcher/collaborators	Practitioner researcher/co-researchers/co-change agents
	Outside researcher as expert/research funding	Client pays an outside consultant – 'they who pay the piper call the tune'	Outside resources and/or internally generated	Outside resources and/or internally generated
	Differentiated roles	Differentiated roles	Merged roles	Shared roles

Action research revisited

References
1. Hart E, Bond M. *Action Research for Health and Social Care. A Guide to Practice.* Buckingham, Open University Press. 1995.
2. Patton MQ. *Qualitative Evaluation and Research Methods.* Thousand Oaks CA, Sage Publications. 1990.
3. Susman GI, Evered RD. An assessment of the scientific merits of action research. *Administrative Science Quarterly.* 1978. 23, 582-603.
4. Meyer J. Stages in the process: a personal account. *Nurse Researcher.* 1995. 2, 3, 24-37.
5. Holter I, Schwartz-Barcott D. Action research: what is it? How has it been used and how can it be used in nursing? *Journal of Advanced Nursing.* 1993. 18, 298-304.
6. Department of Health. *A vision for the future: the nursing, midwifery and health visiting contribution to health care.* HMSO, London. 1993.
7. Carr W, Kemmis S. *Becoming critical: Education, Knowledge and Action Research.* Lewes, The Falmer Press. 1986.
8. Greenwood J. Action research: a few details, a caution and something new. *Journal of Advanced Nursing.* 1994. 20. 13-18.
9. Newton CA. Action research: application in practice. *Nurse Researcher.* 1995. 2, 3, 60-71.
10. Hart E. Action research as a professionalizing strategy: issues and dilemmas. *Journal of Advanced Nursing.* 1996. 23, 454-461.
11. Oiler Boyd C. Towards a nursing practice research method. *Advances in Nursing Science.* 1993. 16, 2, 9-25.
12. Hendry C, Farley AH. The nurse teacher as action researcher. *Nurse Education Today.* 1996. 16, 193-198.
13. Lyon J. *Implementing clinical supervision into an acute care setting: an action research study.* MSc Thesis. Unpublished. University of Manchester. 1997.
14. Benner P. *From Novice to Expert: Excellence and Power in Clinical Nursing Practice.* Menlo Park CA, Addison-Wesley. 1984.
15. Meyer J. New paradigm research in practice: the trials and tribulations of action research. *Journal of Advanced Nursing.* 1993. 18, 1066-1072.
16. Leddy S, Pepper JM. The professional nurse as a change agent. In Leddy S and Pepper JM (Eds). *Conceptual Bases of Professional Nursing.* Second edition. Philadelphia PA, Lippincott. 1989.
17. Tross G, Cavanagh SJ. Innovation in nursing management: professional, management and methodological considerations. *Journal of Nursing Management.* 1996. 4, 143-149.
18. Jarvis P. Reflective practice and nursing. *Nurse Education Today.* 1992. 12, 174-181.

Action research revisited

Keeping above the surface in an action research study

Carol Marrow MPhil, BA(Hons), DPNS, CertEd, RMN, RGN, is Senior Lecturer, Department of Nursing Studies, University College of St Martin, Furness General Hospital, Barrow-in-Furness.

Carol Marrow reflects on her experiences of leading an action research project.

Action research is one of the new paradigm research approaches, which originates from a different perspective than more traditional types of research. It involves doing things with people rather than on people, and aims to professionalise and empower the individuals participating (1), therefore enabling them to change practice. Furthermore, the advancement of knowledge and the improvement of human welfare is considered best achieved through strong links between the research and practice (1-5). Some supporters of research strategies that enable changes in conditions to occur, use the term 'praxis'. One definition of this notion is that it is a commitment to 'knowledge for' or to change behaviours or practice and not only to study it (6). Kemmis (7) wrote about 'praxis' in terms of reflective practice and stated that the outcome of reflection is praxis, 'informed, committed action'. This is one of the important criteria for action research, that the outcomes of the work inform, intelligently, practice. It is argued in this paper, that to enable informed practice to take place

Action research revisited

requires specific criteria related to action research studies.

Through the research referred to in this paper (the background to the study is summarised at the end of the article), I have identified three criteria that help to facilitate essential practice outcomes and these criteria are the basis of the current discussion. These are that:

● Action research is developmental for the participants (participant development)

● Action research is a process of continuous interaction, members of the study collaborate on issues and actions (interaction and collaboration)

● Action research is a continuous process of evaluation by both the participants and the researcher (a continuous process of evaluation).

If these criteria are adopted and are rigorously adhered to throughout the process of the research, then enlightened changes to practice should result.

Participant development

Preparing protocols for action Although preparation of those involved in the research process could be considered under the second criteria of collaboration, for clarity it will be discussed separately as part of the development strategy for the project participants. Furthermore, the term preparation is not necessarily synonymous with collaboration and although there is a strong link to the collaborative aspect of the work, as highlighted, it focuses more on the development of the research participants and research facilitator throughout the study. Indeed, one of the key aims of this project was the personal and professional development of those involved, the notion of preparing participants in all aspects of the research is considered an essential feature of action research studies (1).

Heron (8) suggested that the participants should agree a contract that bring three important strands into being, that of preparation, decision-making and integration, which are to help empower those involved and illustrate the importance of their role in the study. It is important to stress the importance of these three concepts at this stage.

Preparation for the study involved the purchase, preparation and dissemination to the participants of relevant literature as well as involvement in protocol design through workshop attendance. Research of any kind about practice or social interactions raises issues about the nature of the relationship between the researcher and those being researched. Rapoport (9) defined action research as taking place 'within a mutually acceptable ethical framework'. Researchers who fail to acknowledge this could be said to be behaving in an exploitive way. At the outset of this research, especially through the workshops, clear ground rules were negotiated and agreed. These were established for the research study and the reflective diaries and, therefore, considered to be an essential development strategy for both the research participants and the project generally. For example, questions based on Edwards and Talbot's key criteria for ethical research (10) were posed to the group for discussion and agreement. On this basis, the group agreed the following:

● The person who is utilising a diary owns the data in that diary. The data will be revealed and shared (for discussion and evaluation with both the research facilitator and the focus group) if the supervisor/supervisee agrees

● Supervisors and supervisees not to name patients (in their reflective diaries) and others are not to be recognised by the way issues are described. The supervisor has not to identify the supervisee

● No other person to edit the data.

The ground rules identified for the reflective diaries were outlined as following:

● This diary is personal to the user

● There may be some issues outlined in the diary that the user wishes to remain private

● These wishes should be respected

● Other issues that are discussed with the supervisor, should, wherever possible, remain confidential unless felt that it/they could be detrimental to other individuals

● These ground rules should be discussed and agreed at the outset of the supervisory sessions.

Even though clear ground rules, including issues of confidentiality, were

Action research revisited

established at the outset of the study, problems became evident after commencement of the work regarding writing about patients and their care in the diaries. The research participants often experienced dilemmas when having to write in their diary about care issues, they felt that putting something in writing made it seem permanent and real. They also expressed concerns relating to their own competencies and what would happen once these inadequacies were recorded. One of the study participants said: 'I have never really written about patients in a personal way, that is, how I feel about the care they have received and how I feel about my skills and interactions with this patient, I know we have care plans and so on, but somehow they don't always seem that personal because it's not about my skills.'

Further concerns were expressed regarding practitioners' recorded reflections being used for litigation purposes. It was agreed that the complete diary should not be taken into the clinical environment and only brief notes would be made on single sheets of paper. Furthermore, the diary should focus on their skills and practices and not on the patients and that the research ground rules alluded to earlier should be adhered to. Keeping diaries is an important part of professional development, but they should be completed in a professional manner. Six months into the study, due to the tension experienced by the practitioners involved, a one-day workshop was organised to help the practitioners feel more comfortable and confident about writing in their diaries.

Throughout the project the participants progressed in the utilisation of their diaries. Many found that they became quite skilled in writing, they were able to write more concisely and pinpoint important issues more easily. This was a crucial part of their development, as nursing has tended to be a culture with little emphasis on the written word. With the strong accent on academic work in nurse education and the importance of linking theory to practice (11, 12), writing tools in the form of diaries, portfolios, logs and so forth, are being encouraged to enable these outcomes to be achieved (13). The importance of writing about practice was emphasised by Walker (14), who suggested that writing brings 'objectivity' to the learning situation by removing it from the haze of 'subjectivity' which can make the experience unclear. Distancing oneself, in the form of the written word, can help to clarify the issue or situation and thus, enable learning and development to take place.

To support the educational and professional development of the participants throughout the study, an emphasis on strong collaboration between each person involved and the research facilitator was essential. This collaboration was enhanced through having in place fairly sound educational and management systems (5). That said, these systems could have been more robust in terms of accessibility for the participants to the research facilitator and the trust nurse manager, who were often not on site. Education and management systems must be in place for action research studies to be effective. The individuals participating in the research need support and encouragement continually (1, 3, 5). One means of providing a forum for interaction and collaboration was the use of focus group interviews. However, these groups did not become established until two months into the project.

Interaction and collaboration

As identified earlier, one of the main criteria for an action research project is that it is a collaborative investigation with the emphasis being on strong involvement of the study participants, whether these are professionals or lay persons (1, 8, 15-17).

As this was a new initiative, the group of participants involved in the study consisted of volunteers, who were keen and well motivated to develop and take the work forward. As they also had similar professional values as a group of practising nurses, they needed to meet regularly and interact as a group to discuss both research and practice issues.

Establishing and implementing the focus groups

Initially, the study commenced as a managerial-type project because the research was a joint initiative between the trust nurse executive and myself, the research facilitator. This management focus was clearly

Action research revisited

identified when the trust nurse executive requested the need for a
steering group and membership included himself, the research facilitator
and the supervisors involved in the research study. Although benefits of
a management-led project may include commitment by senior personnel
to the findings being supported in action, these advantages of conducting
the research from a position of influence in the establishment, may be
offset by perceptions of the groups lower in the hierarchy that the
research is too closely associated with senior managers (1).

In reflections noted in my personal diary, I began to feel uneasy about
the notion of a steering group, as a steering group is a management tool
to monitor and evaluate a particular issue or intervention in order to
identify cause and effect some action. Individuals often come into a
research project with their own agenda and this is often the case with
management representatives, who are focused on the research outcomes
therefore not always in tune with the key principles of the research
process. The very indication that a management tool is being utilised
could inhibit the research participants. Collaboration is fundamental to
action research and my concern was that participants may experience
repressive feelings through a management-led group.

The first steering group meeting was held one month into the study
and evolved into general discussions about the project. At the second
steering group meeting I asked the supervisors involved in the research
how they saw this group developing; many saw it as a means of support
for them. I also saw it as a valuable means of data collection, therefore
we redefined the ground rules orally, and the group become a focus
group that aimed to give support and by centering on the research
participants' narratives, evaluated the process and outcome of clinical
supervision. Macleod Clark et al (16) stated that if groups are run with
minimal facilitator involvement, or, in other words, are non-management
led, they focus on the research participants, using their agenda, their
language and their frameworks for understanding the world. These are
key requisites of collaborative research.

At this second group meeting, it was also decided that there should be a separate group for the supervisees. This was decided on the basis that any hierarchy in groups can be detrimental to group interactions by inhibiting the lower status individuals (16). This idea was put to the supervisees, who readily agreed to the benefits of separate discussions. Some difficulties were experienced in this division of groups, not least the separate discussion of mutual issues, as benefits could have been drawn from the two groups exploring key issues together, as in practice these issues affected both parties.

Designing and completing the repertory grid

Further evidence of continual participant interaction and collaboration was contained in the designing of the repertory grids. Eight participants from the research sample of 20 were interviewed, and the key themes that came from the interview data were used to design the grid format (18, 19). This grid format included ten elements (clinical learning situations) and ten constructs (the ways the research participants perceived they learnt in the clinical learning situations). Each construct had to be rated on a scale of one to five against each element. Further evidence of collaboration was in letting the participants themselves complete the grid; this helped them to feel that they were in control and not being led by the researcher. This is not the usual activity in grid completion; the interviewer generally fills in the grid based on the participants' oral ratings. In addition, the participants were not just 'researched on' by rating the elements and constructs in the grid, but completion of the grid was followed up with conversation to allow them to reflect on their own use of constructs and situations.

This method of data collection, coupled with the focus group interviews, was part of the means of continually evaluating the research project. The other important evaluation tools were the skills of reflection and continuous analysis of all aspects of the research project. This was enhanced by the use of reflective diaries.

A continuous process of evaluation

Extracts from personal diary As indicated earlier, as principal researcher I felt it was important to keep a reflective diary, and this

Action research revisited

process helped me to evaluate both the research process, or as Holloway (20) called it, the 'audit trail', and my involvement in the study, a key essential in qualitative studies. Care had to be taken so that participants' beliefs and values could be heard above mine. The difficulties encountered with this type of research is the subjectivity of the researcher; many would argue that there is no such thing as a pure or unbiased piece of research, even the choice of topic is often dependent on the researcher's preferences and past experiences (20). For example in this research study, I had a history of professional interest in the clinical support of student and qualified nurses, and Lincoln and Guba (21) believed that the researcher's perceptions can be acknowledged in the research, but that they should not dominate. This sometimes can be difficult as the participants may see you as the expert in that particular field and subsequently look to you for advice and inspiration. This can also have an effect on the validity of the project, especially if the emphasis is from your perspective and not the participants'.

However, a degree of reflexivity on the part of the researcher in any study is crucial if bias is to be reduced to a minimum. Reason and Heron (22) suggested that reflexivity is 'critical subjectivity' in which knowledge is not unthinkingly accepted, but based on critical awareness. Therefore, self-consciousness and critical reflection of the researcher's motives is essential and should take into account the effects of the researcher on the research methods and the findings of the study. In other words, reflecting on aspects of the research process and how the researcher has influenced both data collection methods and interpretation of data is essential.

Through the process of recording my feelings and interpretations on events and issues in my reflective diary, I was able to be more critical about the research process. Some extracts from the diary are given in Box 1.

Kemmis (7) discussed at length the notion of reflection and proposed that reflection can help to make problem solving more efficient and productive, and to make practical discussion wiser and clearer, so critical

Box 1. Extracts from researcher's reflective diary.

● *'How did I feel and perform in todays focus group? Perhaps I was a little impatient when they digressed from talking about clinical supervision. However, I think I am becoming skilled at bringing them back to focus. This has been excellent development for me in group work and group dynamics. I do however, need to be quieter and less controlling. It felt as if I was being too authoritative, but perhaps it was because they kept digressing! It is important to keep focused but I have to take care that I do not lead them where I feel they should go, on analysis of the earlier focus groups transcripts, I feel I may have been guilty of this. I also felt it was imperative not to be oppressive in the groups but to let them feel that they were in control I have found this difficult.'*

● *'Perhaps I need to analyse the interactions in the focus groups more carefully. I read a useful article today on focus groups. What I have been doing is taking individual statements rather then looking at them in the context of the group. Jane talked at length toady about her problems with the supervision, what I really need to do is not just focus on Jane's narrative but the reactions to it from the rest of the group both verbal and non-verbal. Macleod Clark et al (16) state that it is the group that is the unit of analysis not individuals in the group.'*

● *'Today I did some interviews with the grids. Some of the supervisees are great they really reflect and analyse the situations. Susan was good, she took time to think and subsequently the interview was well over an hour. But Louise ticks the boxes very quickly and I'm not sure how deeply she thinks about it. The problem is getting them to complete the grid in the work situation, they often know they have little time to spare because of the ward work and so they try to complete the grid quickly. How valid the ratings on the grids are on these occasions is questionable. I need to try and interview them away from the clinical environment. But would this affect my access to them?'*

Action research revisited

reflection may be improved by our developing deeper analyses of social situations which enclose our reflection and by examining the results of our reflective action for ourselves and others. Writing in my diary and analysing both my feelings and aspects of the study continuously, has helped me not only to evaluate critically the research process, but also identify strengths and weaknesses in both my skills and intentions. It is important to be aware of your effect (as the researcher) on all aspects of the research process and I concur with Kemmis and suggest that this process of reflection has strengthened the research project in terms of its validity and to some degree its reliability. In terms of validity, it has promoted a change in the participants and their practice that is real and appropriate to the context in which the new initiative (clinical supervision) was implemented and studied. In terms of reliability, the findings from this work have been made more dependable by the presentation of information that has been analysed continuously and reflected on critically, resulting in evidence that is true.

Evaluating the focus groups

To take this discussion forward, through the reflective process, the participants, especially the supervisees, had identified and were quite open about sensitive care issues in their focus groups. On occasions they alluded to poor care practices and it was agreed that these would not be taken out of the group and that it was the responsibility of those involved to deal with them. There is a danger of damaging the continuation of research projects if practice issues are handled insensitively. That said, from experience gained from an observation study carried out a few years ago (23-25), I am convinced that professional issues should take priority over research initiatives and it is how the situation is dealt with that is more important. There are, however, various schools of thought on this notion. One particular strand was proposed by Bogdan and Taylor (26) who suggested that some researchers believe that passively to observe behaviour and not intervene, is to condone that behaviour. Conversely, other researchers accept that intervention could change behaviours and therefore affect the study (27). They also agree that there is the chance of the researcher losing credibility and being refused further access. Nevertheless, there are ways of keeping the research project intact and at the same time resolving professional issues; it is about being sensitive. This important issue is illustrated in an extract from my diary: 'One of the research participants arrived at my office door today in an extremely emotional state. She relayed the trauma she had recently experienced in the work environment. In a clinical supervision session she had shared something personal relating to her practice. Later she heard the recipient of her confidence discussing the issue with other work colleagues. As the research facilitator, she felt that I should sort the problem out by talking to the person involved. We explored this problem and agreed that she should deal with the problem in the next supervisory session. The enormity of this breach in confidentiality was analysed in terms of the Code of Professional Conduct (28) and if a confidentiality between associates can be broken so easily, then so could a confidence between nurse and patient. The situation was eventually resolved, the participants did discuss the situation and the guilty person apologised. My concern was that if this incident had not happened in a research project would it have been resolved? How often do situations like this occur, either between colleagues or nurses and patients? Further, if I had handled the situation differently by intervening, would it have jeopardised their involvement in the research project?'

Through continuous reflection and maintaining my diary in this study, I now realise the importance of very detailed and clearly articulated rules for any research project, and especially action research due to the very complexity of its nature. Reflection, according to Kemmis (7), is 'meta thinking', that is, thinking about thinking. In doing this we consider the connection between our thoughts and action in a focused situation. This helps to reason out the relationship between our thoughts and our actions in order to further and deepen our thinking, and thus, understand the objective meaning behind the action. This deeper thinking process can also have negative effects on the individuals involved. As highlighted by the group evaluations, sensitive issues can be illuminated, although as

Action research revisited

Kemmis suggested, this illumination of issues will in the long-term help to improve practice and in the nursing situation, improve standards of patient care. An example from this study could help to illustrate this point. A supervisee in the focus group talked at length about an issue that was very troubling for her: 'A doctor would not come out to certify a death, I kept phoning him and he said I can't come now, can night sister do it? I replied no, the night sisters do not certify death. I rang the doctor later as he still hadn't come, he apparently was having his supper and his absence continued. I later wrote it down in my diary as it bothered me, I know I did the right thing by persisting and not allowing the patient to be taken away without certification.'; 'I later reflected on it and had a word with the doctor. I also discussed it with my clinical supervisor and she said I did the right thing by not letting the lady off the ward without being certified.'

This research participant felt, that reflecting and discussing this sensitive issue helped her to put the problem in perspective and increase her confidence for future dealings in similar situations.

Conclusion

Some experiences of leading and participating in an action research study have been highlighted and discussed here. The main issues considered include the importance of facilitating the preparation and development of those involved and collaborating with them on all aspects of the research process. Furthermore, critical reflections on the part of the researcher, coupled with sensitivity to shared knowledge and practice issues have been crucial to the successful continuation of the work.

The enormity of executing this kind of study can not be underestimated; it has been one of the most complex and challenging experiences in the whole of my professional career. At times I felt I was drowning in a sea of people and data; at other times, when sharing knowledge and expertise with the other participants, I felt incredibly humble. Although complex, action research is an important initiative for developing nursing practice. Through systematic and rigorous critical reflection and sharing of issues, nurses can achieve optimum results in terms of their professional development and resulting practice.

Summary

Practitioner research and more specifically action research, requires the individual researcher to become actively involved in the research experience. Like nursing, this type of research shows respect for subjectivity by sharing or giving back to the individual rather than 'doing research on them'. In other words it is an interactional, mutually respecting experience.

In this paper, through the process of the research participants' reflections, the principles and complexities of action research have been explored.

Three important criteria for action research have been identified:
● Participant development
● Interaction and collaboration
● A continuous process of evaluation.

These three criteria have been discussed in relation to one research project. The study explored the concepts of clinical supervision and reflective practice with the intention of measuring participants' professional development through the process of clinical supervision. The research involved six case studies, six nurses as clinical supervisors and 14 nurses as supervisees.

The data was collected over an eighteen month period using structured interviews based on the repertory grid technique, semi-structured interviews and focused group discussions. The individual participants maintained a reflective diary to help them critically appraise their practice.

As a participant in the research, I also maintained a reflective diary to help me explore my development as both an action researcher and an educationalist. This diary has helped me to understand the complexities of action research and the notion of the researcher 'being immersed' in the research relationships.

The experiences have suggested that action research is a complex process, but a vital initiative for developing nurses and their practice.

Action research revisited

References.

1. Hart E, Bond M. *Action Research For Health and Social Care: A Guide to Practice.* Buckingham, Open University Press. 1995.

2. Chaiklin S. Understanding the social scientific practice of understanding practice. In Chaiklin S, Lave J (Eds). *Understanding Practice: Perspectives on Activity and Context.* Cambridge, Cambridge University Press. 1993.

3. Meyer J. New paradigm research in practice: the trials and tribulations of action research. *Journal of Advanced Nursing.* 1993. 18, 1066-1072.

4. Rolfe G. *Expanding Nursing Knowledge: Understanding and Researching your own Practice.* Oxford, Butterworth and Heinemann. 1998.

5. Webb C. Action research: philosophy, methods and personal experiences. *Journal of Advanced Nursing.* 1989. 14, 403-410.

6. Stanley L. *Feminist Praxis.* London, Routledge Press. 1990.

7. Kemmis S. Action research and the politics of reflection. In Boud D *et al.* (Eds) *Reflection: Turning Experience Into Learning.* London, Kogan Page. 1985.

8. Heron J. *Co-operative Inquiry: Research into the Human Condition.* London, Sage. 1996.

9. Rapoport R. Three dilemmas in action research. *Human Relations.* 23, 6, 499-513.

10. Edwards A, Talbot R. *The Hard-pressed Researcher: A Research Handbook for the Caring Professions.* London, Longman Press. 1994.

11. Kitson A. *Nursing Art and Science.* London, Chapman & Hall. 1993.

12. Slevin O, Basford L. *Theory and Practice of Nursing: An Integrated Approach To Patient Care.* Edinburgh, Campion Press. 1995.

13. English National Board. *Standards for Approval of Higher Education Institutions and Programmes.* London, ENB. 1998.

14. Walker D. Writing and reflection. In Boud D *et al.* (Eds) *Reflection: Turning Experience Into Learning.* London, Kogan Page. 1985.

15. Reason P, Rowen J (Eds). *Human Inquiry: A Sourcebook of New Paradigm Research.* Chichester, John Wiley & Sons. 1981.

16. Macleod Clark J *et al.* The use of focus group interviews in nursing research: issues and challenges. *NT Research.* 1996. 1, 2, 143-152.

17. Morgan DL. *Focus Groups as Qualitative Research.* Second edition. Qualitative Research Methods Series 16. London, Sage. 1997.

18. Fransella F, Bannister D. *A Manual For Repertory Grid Technique.* London, Academic Press. 1977.

19. Stewart V, Stewart A. *Business Application of Repertory Grid.* London, McGraw-Hill Book Company (UK) Ltd. 1981.

20. Holloway I. *Basic Concepts for Qualitative Research.* Abingdon, Blackwell Science. 1997.

21. Lincoln YS, Guba EG. *Naturalistic Inquiry.* Newbury Park CA, Sage. 1985.

22. Reason P, Heron J. Cooperative inquiry. In Smith JA *et al* (Eds). *Rethinking Methods in Psychology.* London, Sage. 1995.

23. Marrow CE, Tatum S. Student supervision: myth or reality. *Journal of Advanced Nursing.* 19, 1247-1255.

24. Marrow CE. *Clinical Supervision in Action: Problems and Dilemmas.* Unpublished MPhil thesis. Lancaster, Lancaster University. 1995.

25. Marrow CE. Using qualitative research methods in nursing. *Nursing Standard.* 1996. 11, 7, 43-45.

26. Bogdan R, Taylor SJ. *Introduction to Qualitative Research Methods: A Phenomenological Approach to the Social Sciences.* New York NY, John Wiley. 1975.

27. Sapsford R, Abbott P. *Research Methods for Nurses and the Caring Professions.* Buckingham, Open University Press. 1992.

28. United Kingdom Central Council for Nursing, Midwifery and Health Visiting. *Code of Professional Conduct.* London, RCN. 1992.

Nursing Standard Publications produces a range of journals in various specialist areas of nursing which include:

Nursing Standard

● The weekly professional journal which keeps you up-to-date with the issues affecting nursing

Elderly Care

● A bi-monthly journal for nurses involved in the care of elderly people

Paediatric Nursing

● A monthly journal for nurses caring for children in hospital and the community

Primary Health Care

● The Royal College of Nursing's official community nursing monthly journal

Nursing Management

● A monthly journal for nurse managers and senior personnel

Emergency Nurse

● The journal of the Royal College of Nursing Accident and Emergency Nursing Association

For subscription details and information on any of these journals, call the Nursing Standard marketing department:

Tel: 0181 423 1066. Fax: 0181 423 4302

or write to: Nursing Standard Publications, Nursing Standard House, 17-19 Peterborough Road, Harrow, Middlesex HA1 2AX.

Issues in research

Managing the 'sensitive' research interview: a personal account

Interviews can be a rich source for data collection, but, maintains Kate Sullivan, researchers must be meticulous in their preparation.

There is a paucity of empirical evidence detailing the phenomenon of bereavement for the partner in a same-sex relationship. Available research and descriptive accounts suggest that faced with real or perceived social sanctions many individuals suffering this traumatic life event feel unable to disclose the magnitude of their grief to others (1-5). The study on which this paper is based described the experience of bereavement for ten men and four women whose partner's death had been caused by a variety of disease processes or by non-accidental means. This paper has been presented as an account of the interview process used to collect data for this study.

Advantages and disadvantages of using interviews
The interview has been described as 'a conversation with a purpose' (6). There are a number of advantages to using this method of data collection. First, the interview takes into consideration those individuals who would be unable or unwilling to write out a long coherent answer. In the study on which this paper is based a number of participants indicated that they would have been unable, either emotionally or physically, to commit their experiences to paper. Second, depending on the research issues to be explored the interview may be the most appropriate way to facilitate an individual to speak freely about their experiences. Third, the interview permits the

interviewer to assess the latent content of the interview, as expressed by facial expressions or by notation, and gives them the opportunity to probe and seek clarification of issues as necessary. The ability to probe, and to focus progressively on the phenomena under study, are two of the essential attributes of qualitative researchers. However, they must always be mindful not to cause any unnecessary harm to the research participant. While qualitative research is considered to be non-invasive, Munhall (7) has commented that that is a limited perception of the word. She suggested that while the researcher does not cause any physical intervention to the participant, there is an invasion of their psyche. For some participants this may be therapeutic, but for others it may produce possible risks to their health. Schrock (8) also thought along these lines and wrote: 'There is little doubt however, that the individual researcher's sensitivity to the moral implications of research and a firm adherence to a professional code of practice are the only foundations on which the security and well-being of all who participate in research, or contribute to it in any form, can rest.'

There are also disadvantages to the use of the research interview. The interview may encourage a verbose individual to wander off the topic. In this case the interviewer must be prepared to guide the interviewee firmly, but politely, back to the subject. Field and Morse (9) alerted the reader to the common pitfalls in interviewing such as:

- Interruptions, usually the telephone or an unexpected caller
- Other distractions, for example, the interviewer not allowing sufficient time for the interview and having to hurry the interviewee
- Stage fright on the part of either the interviewer or the interviewee, especially when an audio-tape of the interview is being made
- The interviewer failing to ask the questions in a logical or coherent fashion
- The interviewer resorting to teaching, preaching, or counselling the interviewee.

It could be concluded from what has been written, that interviews are an indispensable means of collecting data involving human beings. However, the method is not totally free from failure. It is the

Issues in research

responsibility of the researcher to take account of the weaknesses, as well as the strengths of this method of data collection, before deciding to use it. The key consideration however, is the potential richness of the data that can be obtained by the use of a personal interview. Massarik (10) wrote of the reciprocity which occurs when the interviewer and the interviewee build up a rapport, and value each other as persons, with genuine motives and feelings. It was decided in the planning of the research study referred to here that an interview would provide the participants with the opportunity to reflect, progressively focus, and elaborate on their experience of bereavement.

Ethical considerations

Smith (11), in her study of alcohol-dependent and problem-drinking women, defined the term 'ethical' as the ability to distinguish between right and wrong, and the researcher's understanding of duty and obligation. She recognised that the development of an individual's ethical position is influenced by his or her attitudes, values and beliefs. **Do no harm** Smith referred to the assertion of Morse (12) that balance is a component of ethical interviewing. Balance is seen as the potential good that may be derived from a research study, matched with the potential harm the study may cause a participant. The complexity of the interview must also be considered. If the focus of the interview is of a sensitive nature, and the participant is disclosing private and intimate information to the researcher (who in the case of this study was a stranger to him or her), the researcher has a responsibility in ethical terms to handle such material with sensitivity and not to probe beyond the limits of the study, or in such a way as to produce, or encourage, greater emotional pain. To interview and then leave someone in emotional distress is morally wrong. Based on my own judgement, I spent time with each participant before the interview commenced, and after it was concluded as I judged this to be the morally 'right' thing to do. Prior to the interviews taking place a number of other issues had to be considered.

Consent from the participants When I appealed for volunteers to take part in the study, 17 people wrote to me indicating their willingness to participate in the study. Another five individuals were contacted by an intermediary who furnished them with my contact address and telephone number. Subsequently, these individuals contacted me by letter or telephone and expressed their willingness to be involved in the study.

When the initial search for volunteers commenced, my name with a contact address at the university was provided. The use of the university address was to assure potential respondents that I was linked to a credible research institution. I also stated that I was a nurse and that the research programme was being funded by a research studentship from the department of health and social services in Northern Ireland. When the initial contact was made by the participant I furnished them with my home address and telephone number to reciprocate the trust that they had placed in me. Further contact was maintained with the participants, in some cases over a period of six months. On each occasion the participant was given the opportunity to withdraw from the study, however, each affirmed their commitment to the study.

Confidentiality I provided each participant with an undertaking that all data/information relating to them, and to their partner, would be kept confidential. They were assured that their names would not appear anywhere in the transcribed material. I advised participants that they were free to choose a pseudonym for themselves and their partner, but if they preferred I would do this for them. Five of the participants welcomed the opportunity to choose their own pseudonyms. In addition it was agreed with the participants that their geographical location would be described in general terms, for example, a city or urban area in Northern Ireland, or a rural area in England. Occupation would also be described only in broad terms.

Other considerations The time, place, and length of the interview was dictated by the participant, who was also free to withdraw from the interview at any time. It was explained to the participants that it would be helpful (to me) if the interviews could be tape-recorded. An undertaking was given that if the participant agreed to the use of an audio-tape to record the interview data, this would be held in

Issues in research

conditions of strict security, and that the tapes would be destroyed following completion of the research programme, or at any other time prior to this, on receipt of their instructions. One participant in the main study requested that his interview was not taped. The decision of the participant in all these matters was final, and was not questioned.

Use of an audio-tape to collect data

Field and Morse (9) gave the researcher some useful hints on the use of this method of data collection. It was with these in mind that I set out to commence the study. Giving due consideration to the fact that the majority of interviews were to be conducted in the participant's home, I was restricted in the layout of the room to be used. However, there were a number of conditions over which I had control.

The importance of an unobtrusive tape-machine and powerful microphone was a priority. A small flat table microphone was obtained, to be used with a previously acquired machine. This proved to be of great benefit. It had an excellent pick-up range, yet was barely noticeable. I used batteries to power the machine for two reasons. In the first place it was deemed improper to use another person's power supply (presuming one existed). Second, it ensured that the machine could be located out of sight, thus reducing potential distraction. Spare batteries and a power lead were always carried as a precaution. Audiotapes were checked before each interview and spare ones brought along to the interview location.

The field test

Polit and Hungler (13) reminded the researcher that because unforeseen problems can arise in the course of a study it is advisable to carry out a trial run prior to commencement of the main study. They suggested that if this does not happen researchers may find themselves with problems so severe that the study may have to be stopped. The aim of the field test (involving three participants) in my study was to discover what practical difficulties might be experienced during the data collection and data analysis stages of the main study. Overall the results of the field test were most favourable with no major difficulties arising.

One important discovery during the field test was the amount of time that required to be spent with each of the participants. Because of the sensitive nature of the interviews, I deemed it necessary to spend some time with the participants prior to and following the interview, an ethical consideration discussed earlier.

The period of time spent with each person varied according to need. However, the shortest time was four hours, and the longest was six hours. The latter included a three-hour interview. In total six hours of taped interviews were obtained from the three participants. The transcription and analysis of these interviews also prepared me for this process after the data collection phase of the main study.

The main study

Participants Four men from Northern Ireland, and ten men and five women from Great Britain, constituted the potential sample for the main study. Regrettably one man from Northern Ireland, and one man from Great Britain died before the research interview could take place. This reduced the study sample to 17 participants.

Data collection The 17 interviews which formed the data collection phase for the main study were conducted over a three-month period. Three of the interviews were conducted in Northern Ireland, and fourteen conducted in Great Britain. The latter took place over a 17-day period, and a subsequent three-day period, since I would have been unable to travel from Northern Ireland to Great Britain on a more frequent basis.

After the initial contact the participants and I made written and, or, verbal contact on at least three occasions prior to the interview. This level of contact was necessary to ensure that the participant continued to be willing to take part in the study, and to negotiate the arrangements for the interview. The latter was particularly important when I was travelling to Great Britain to conduct interviews. I had to balance the need to build rapport with the participants with the

Issues in research

possible risk of inducing participant dependence upon me as a 'counsellor'. However, this did not appear to happen, and I was treated with the utmost courtesy and consideration by all the participants who were co-operative and easy to interview.

The ethical considerations described earlier were adhered to at all times. Where possible in the interview situation I positioned myself so that I and the participant sat at right angles to each other, able to maintain eye contact, yet not close enough for the situation to appear threatening; each chair was of the same height, and I ensured, where possible, that no other piece of furniture formed a barrier between us. Every attempt was made to ensure that the participants were as much at ease as possible. A number of sources suggest that the best way to put another person at ease is to be at ease yourself. This I endeavoured to do. Also individuals are more likely to be candid with the person who appears honest and non-judgemental. I did not detect any unease or suspicion among the participants.

One way of ensuring that each participant was at ease in the interview situation, was to encourage each individual to decide where the interview would take place. Two of the Northern Ireland participants opted to be interviewed at home, as did ten of the participants in Great Britain. One of the Northern Ireland participants elected to be interviewed at my university base. This was because of family commitments (the presence of an elderly parent). Four of the participants in Great Britain chose to be interviewed in the home of a friend. This arrangement was to 'ensure privacy', or because the participant deemed it to be 'more convenient'.

I met the three Northern Ireland participants and four of the 14 participants from Great Britain at the interview venue. The other ten participants from Great Britain chose to meet me at a neutral venue, (in most cases the railway or coach station), and then proceed to the interview base. In our final communication before the interview each gave the other a detailed personal description in order to prevent confusion or embarrassment. This plan worked well, and we recognised each other without any difficulty.

The time spent together before the interview commenced was used to reiterate the purpose of the research. It was also used by the participant and myself as a time when we could relax, often over a cup of coffee, and get to know each other. Various topics were discussed, from my journey, and the merits and demerits of the British transport system, to the ongoing concern among homosexual men about the series of murders taking place in the London area. Usually this pre-interview period lasted about one hour. There were variations of about 15 minutes on either side. The participant indicated, as previously requested by me, when they were ready to start the interview.

Consideration of the needs of the participant was paramount during the interview. Two of the participants became very distressed when describing the illness and or death of their partner. At this juncture the interview was suspended and the individual given the option to withdraw from the interview. Neither of the participants took up this option, though one man indicated that if he had realised 'how hard' it was going to be, he would not have volunteered to take part in the study.

Prior to the commencement of the interviews I had made a decision that if the interviews became too distressing for the participants, then I would bring the interview to a close. As in all other aspects of dealing with human beings I had to be prepared to take a moral stand and, if necessary, justify my actions as the right and proper thing to do. To do otherwise could be construed as unethical. My role was not to produce a catharsis, but the discussion of such an emotional event as the death of a loved person sometimes did produce this. As described above, two of the participants became distressed when discussing their partner's death and the interview was suspended. Also a number of participants cried at different times during the research interview, but did not want the interview suspended. At the forefront of my mind was always the thought that to be permitted a private view of another person's past, their pain, and their sorrow, was a privilege.

A further consideration had to be made in relation to providing emotional support for any of the participants who might have required it after the interview was concluded. At the time of the research study I

Issues in research

had been a nurse for 25 years. I had also undertaken a course in bereavement counselling, and felt able to make a reasonable judgement as to the emotional condition of the participant after completion of the interview. However, provision was made for support to be made available for each individual if required. In some cases this would have been provided by health or social care professionals already involved with the individual, by someone involved with a voluntary agency from whom the individual was already receiving support, or by a friend. These arrangements were made prior to the date of the interview, and with the full consent of the participant.

In the event, none of the participants requested anything over and above the time I spent with them at the conclusion of the interview, and reliance upon their 'normal' support network. The time spent with each participant after the interview was concluded was dictated by the participant . On a number of occasions participants requested that I have refreshments and a 'chat', before leaving their home. I believed that to have refused this offer of hospitality could have been perceived as ungracious.

As well as the former considerations, the time spent with the participants was valuable for the purpose of the research. Perhaps because the participants were relaxed, having completed the 'formal' interview, which ranged in length from one hour to three hours, some of them added other pieces of information to that which they had already given. I checked with the participant whether it was acceptable to include this with the taped data. On two occasions the participant requested that this information was not used in the research. I honoured that request, and those disclosures do not form any part of the research data. When permission to include this material was given, I made notes which were included in the subsequent data for that participant. I wrote to each participant after the interview and thanked them for their participation in the study.

It is almost inevitable that when a volunteer sample is sought some people who say they meet the criteria for inclusion in the study, but do not, will offer to take part. In this situation secondary selection (12) can be employed. This strategy can be implemented in one of two ways. Either the interview can be stopped, or the researcher can decide to continue with the interview and exclude the data from the study. I would argue that when the research is of a sensitive nature as was the case in the present study, and gaining access to the sample had been difficult (14), it was better to continue with the interview and employ the process of secondary selection at the transcription stage of the research process. This was the strategy I adopted with regard to three of the 17 participants who volunteered to take part in the study, but who at the time of interview clearly demonstrated that they did not meet the criterion laid down for inclusion in the study. Interview data from the remaining fourteen participants provided me with 24.5 hours of taped material, as well as one and a half hours of notes from the interview that was not taped.

Issues of a personal nature
Particular problems can arise for the researcher who appeals for volunteers in a journal, newspaper, or through a radio programme, as was the case in this study. I found myself going to meet with unknown individuals, usually on unknown territory. This can be a somewhat 'daunting' experience for any researcher, but perhaps more so for a lone female. The problem seemed less difficult when the interviews were being conducted in Northern Ireland as this is my home. Even though I travelled by car to conduct these interviews I was still conscious of going into 'sensitive' areas as a stranger. This might seem a strange statement to someone not familiar with the civil unrest that has existed in Northern Ireland for almost 30 years. For those who are not aware of these issues a 'sensitive' area is one where the movement of unknown persons or vehicles are closely monitored

Meticulous attention was paid to the detailed travel arrangements for the study in Great Britain. The interviews were conducted in the summer, when the daylight hours were longer. At one stage during the planning of the research I considered using my own transport to travel to the interview venue. However, when I weighed up the advantages

Issues in research

and disadvantages of this over the use of public transport, the latter was chosen as a preferred alternative. I was not familiar with many of the areas that I would be visiting. This could have been a potential stressor which was best avoided. I therefore decided that it was better to arrive at the interview relaxed. It also freed me on the return journey to reflect on the days work, and to 'de-brief' myself in preparation for the next day's interview.

Consideration also had to be given to a further issue. In the months leading up to the period of the first cohort of research interviews in Great Britain (July 1993) a number of men who identified as homosexual had been murdered. Indeed the week prior to the commencement of the study a fifth man had been murdered. While, as a female, this was not a major personal worry for me, apart from my concern for those who had been killed and their loved ones, it was considered judicious that someone should be aware of my travel plans. This like all other aspects of my personal safety was discussed with my supervisor.

We agreed that the best way to deal with this situation was that he and my host (a family friend) would each hold a detailed itinerary of where I was at any given time. These details would be held under secure conditions in a marked and sealed envelope by the two individuals concerned. My host was also provided with a list of my expected time of arrival back to base each day together with details of what action to take if I failed to arrive back, or make telephone contact, within one hour of this time. The agreed procedure was that she would contact my supervisor and he would make the decision as to what further action was necessary. Consideration had been given to the possible involvement of other agencies to secure my safety. However, after lengthy deliberation it was agreed that the risk to the confidentiality of the research participants was too great. I was fortunate that nothing untoward occurred during the period that the interviews were conducted. The sealed envelopes remained sealed, and were handed back to me when the interviews were completed. They were subsequently destroyed.

While physical safety is paramount for any researcher, those persons who engage in a study dealing with highly emotive issues must ensure that their psychological safety is addressed. As the interviews in this study were often distressing for the participant, this in some measure had an effect on me. This exposure to pain and grief was re-awakened during the transcription and analysis stage of the research. At times during the transcription of the taped interviews the pain being experienced by the participants was almost tangible. I constantly reminded myself during this time that I might require support to help me deal with these issues. Dunn (15) reminded the reader that to continue with research when one is suffering emotionally because of it would be unethical. I was fortunate in the respect that I was able, to the best of my knowledge, to deal with the issues myself.

Preparing data for analysis

I elected to transcribe the interview tapes myself for three reasons. First, I gave the participants an assurance that I would maintain the anonymity of all data/information relating to them, and to their partner. The participants did, however, consent to my supervisor having access to the interview tapes. Part of the assurance given to the participants was that neither their, or their partners' name, would appear in the transcribed material; instead a pseudonym would be used. In addition, it was agreed that their geographical location and occupation would be described in broad terms only. In order to meet these undertakings I believed that the responsibility for transcription of the interview tapes should not be delegated to a third party.

Second, describing the events surrounding the death of a loved person can be very painful and distressing. Emotions expressed by the participants during the interview must in some measure have an effect on the researcher. This exposure to pain and grief may also occur during transcription of the interviews. Consequently, I believed that it would be unfair to expect another person to deal with such potentially traumatic encounters.

Third, in order to have as much exposure to the interview data as possible I believed that it was important for me to be involved actively

Issues in research

in the transcription process. While this proved to be a difficult and lengthy exercise for a novice audio-typist (the interviews which were transcribed verbatim amounted to almost 250,000 words), it enabled me to become acquainted intimately with the data. During the transcription of each interview I included information relating to such things as sighing, pauses in the conversation, inflections, tone of voice, or the expression of emotions such as laughter or tears. Each participant's interview was allocated a discrete file, and labelled with the participant's pseudonym. This enabled me to identify clearly and separate each participant's response and also ensure that their identity was not revealed to anyone . When each research interview was transcribed I made a second copy of the disk, which, for reasons of security, was stored in a separate location.

Conclusion

This paper has been presented as a personal account of how I managed the interview process when undertaking what could be considered sensitive research. Not all researchers, even those dealing with emotive issues, will be presented with many of the potential problems I encountered. It is to those who will face these challenges, or more difficult ones, that I have presented this paper. I hope that making the process as transparent as possible will be helpful to them. Finally, I would wish to leave the reader with some personal thoughts. This study has been a privilege for me. I have had the unique experience of sharing the most private and innermost thoughts of the participants. As I transcribed and analysed the data, these almost tangible and very humbling experiences were relived. As Morse and Field (16) noted: 'Doing qualitative research is an intense experience. It enriches one's life; it captures one's soul and intellect.'

Kate Sullivan PhD, BSc(Hons), RGN, RCNT, DN(London), RNT, is a lecturer in nursing, School of Health Sciences, University of Ulster at Jordanstown, Newtownabbey, Co Antrim.

References.

1. Weinbach RW. Sudden death and secret survivors: helping those who grieve alone. *Social Work.* 1989. 34, 1, 57 -60.

2. Wertheimer A. Mourning in secret. *New Society.* 1987. 17, 8-9.

3. Siegal RA, Hoefer DD. Bereavement counselling for gay individuals. *American Journal of Psychotherapy.* 1981. 35, 4, 517-525.

4. Klein SJ, Fletcher W. Gay grief. An examination of its uniqueness brought to light by the AIDS crisis. *Journal of Psychosocial Oncology.* 1986. 4, 3, 15-25.

5. Bronski M. Death and the erotic imagination. *Radical America.* 1987. 21, 2-3, 59-60.

6. Kahn R, Cannell C. *The Dynamics of Interviewing.* New York NY, John Wiley. 1957.

7. Munhall PL. Institutional review of qualitative research proposals: a task of no small consequence. In Morse JM (Ed). *Qualitative Nursing Research: A Contemporary Dialogue.* London, Sage Publications Ltd. 1991.

8. Schrock R. Moral issues in nursing research. In Cormack DFS (Ed). *The Research Process in Nursing.* Second edition. Oxford, Blackwell Scientific Publications. 1991.

9. Field PA, Morse JM. *Nursing Research: The Application of Qualitative Approaches.* London, Croom Helm. 1985.

10. Massarik F. The interviewing process re-examined. In Reason P, Rowan J (Eds). *Human Inquiry: A Sourcebook of New Paradigm Research.* Chichester, John Wiley and Sons. 198 1.

11. Smith L. Ethical issues in interviewing. *Journal of Advanced Nursing.* 1992. 17, 9, 98-102.

12. Morse JM. *Qualitative Nursing Research: A Contemporary Dialogue.* London, Chapman Hall. 1991.

13. Polit DF, Hungler BP. *Essentials of Nursing Research Methods, Appraisal and Utilization.* Second edition. London, Lippincott Company. 1989.

14. Sullivan K. Experiences with a volunteer sample. *Nurse Researcher.* 1996. 3, 4, 69-76.

15. Dunn L. Pearls, pith and provocation, research alert! Qualitative research may be hazardous to your health!. *Qualitative Health Research.* 1991. 1, 3, 388-392.

16. Morse JM, Field PA. *Nursing Research: The Application of Qualitative Approaches.* Second edition. London, Chapman and Hall. 1996.

Issues in research

Do computers have value in the data collection process for nurse researchers?

Computer technology offers time and resource saving opportunities for researchers, even for the most menial of tasks, suggest the authors.

This paper discusses whether computers have a place in data collection for nurse researchers. It describes the use made of computers and the Internet to manage the data collection stage of a research study which examined if gender affects nurse teachers' attitudes to information technology (IT). Nurse teachers were surveyed from eight institutions of nursing education, one randomly chosen from each region in England. The authors conclude that the computer can be a great asset to the nurse researcher if used appropriately.

Computers – people tend to like or loathe them. In the authors' experience, nurse researchers are no different from the rest of the population in this respect. There is a continuum of computer usage from those who delight in the speed with which computers can analyse their data to others who would not even trust the computer to store data, let alone assist in drawing any conclusions from them. Do computers then, really have value for nurse researchers in the data collection process or is it just the domain of 'computer techies'? This paper examines the question and considers the use made of computers during the data collection stage of a research study which examined if gender affects nurse teachers' attitudes to IT.

The survey

Nurse teachers were surveyed from eight institutions of nursing education, one randomly chosen from each region in England. Teacher establishment data indicated the total number of teachers employed as being nearly 5,000 within 50 institutions. This meant that approximately 800 teaching staff would be surveyed.

In order to carry out the survey, heads of the chosen eight institutions were contacted for permission to approach staff and to obtain a staff list. Once obtained each subject was then contacted with an introductory letter and a summary of the study protocol. The letter also contained details of where the full study protocol could be found on the World Wide Web (Web). This was followed a few days later by another letter together with the survey questionnaire and a stamped addressed envelope for the reply. For those who did not reply within the stipulated time-frame, a follow-up letter and another copy of the survey questionnaire was sent out. In a worst case scenario of receiving no replies to the initial mailing, this could have meant dealing with 8,000 items; three letters + three envelopes + two survey questionnaires + one protocol summary + one return envelope = ten items x 800 individuals. No clerical support was available for the study, which meant that one person carried out the bulk of the work. Ways of automating processes had to be found.

Possible manual solutions Before the use of computers became so widespread, this study would probably have progressed in a very different manner from that described above. The introductory letter, protocol summary, main letter, survey and follow-up letter would have been typed up on a typewriter and photocopied to produce the numbers required. With such limited manpower personalisation of the letters to 'Dear Jo' and 'Dear Fred' would have been out of the question.

Mailing would probably have been achieved by typing up names and addresses in an appropriate layout and then photocopying onto labels for each of the three mailings. As with all documents produced on a typewriter, any mistake that was not found in time for the corrector ribbon would have meant retyping the whole page again.

Issues in research

To reduce postage costs, bundles of envelopes would be sent together to a school or site address for distribution to staff pigeonholes. To assist distribution it would be helpful to sort the envelopes alphabetically for each site. Great care would need to be taken when typing the labels to achieve this if a manual sort was to be prevented.

Reminders would probably not have been sent out. If they were, they would have been sent to everyone, as it would have been very time-consuming to filter out manually those who had already replied. A check would be needed of the return list against the printed labels to remove those not required.

Computer solutions

In this research the computer was very much in evidence to provide solutions to the lack of manpower available.

Mail merge Mail merge enables personalised letters and documents to be sent to people in a mailing list. Two files are created. The main document contains the text that will be sent to each recipient. It also contains codes to indicate where to insert the information from the mailing list. The mailing list, often called the data source, contains the information about the people that the main document will be sent to. Data is stored in fields, chunks of information, so that each field can be inserted in different places in the main document. This is similar to an address book where different information is entered for name, address and telephone number.

For the study Microsoft$^®$ Office 97 was used. Office 97 is a suite of programs that are able to interact together. Word 97 is the word-processor in the suite. The Tools menu in Word 97 takes you through the steps needed to create the main document, link it to or create a data source and run the merge. Word 97 also suggests fields for the data source when you create it (Fig. 1). Unless other specific fields are needed these will probably suffice.

The first use of mail merge in the study was to contact the eight heads of institutions for permission to approach their staff. Admittedly mail

Figure 1. Creating a data source.

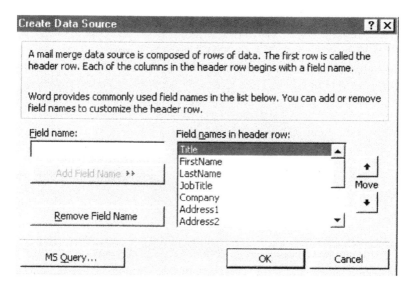

merge does not really save any time for such a small mailing list, however, in the spirit of the study it was thought appropriate to use the technology where applicable.

In the main, the response from the institutions was to send a hard copy list of staff with contact details. One institution, however, sent their list in an Excel file and this was then transferred field by field into the Word data file. The paper lists had to be typed into the data file. Some institutions simply sent a copy of their full staff list. Details of non-teaching staff were excluded. Some job titles could debatably indicate posts held by nurse teachers and were included. A total of 767 names were included from eight institutions.

Using mail merge undoubtedly saved time. It also enabled personalised letters to be sent which would otherwise have been impossible. It did take time to type the names into the computer, but even simply producing labels would have required this. To save time with printing, template letters were photocopied, with space left in appropriate places. The photocopies were then fed into the printer and the main document was prepared to merge details into the spaces. To

Issues in research

ensure the information was in the correct place on the page, text boxes were used.

Output can be sorted while performing a merge. This was very useful for printing out the data in university, school, site, last name order. Letters sent to a central distribution point within a school/site were thus already sorted alphabetically to be put in the internal post and then into staff pigeonholes.

One solution that was not used would have been to scan the printed lists. In order to read them into the data source however would have required work on each list to manipulate it into the format needed. As no two lists were in the same format it was felt to be quicker to simply type them in.

With all data entry a second person was used as 'checker' to ensure the accuracy of the data. There was little point in trying to send a personalised letter to 'Dear Jo' when it should have been 'Dear Joe'.

Random number generation Every subject in the data set was allocated a random number. Word does not have the facility to allocate these. The researchers did however have access to a program that generates numbers at random. The program asks for the number required, and the lowest and highest number. A margin of error of 200 above the expected 800 was allowed for. Thus 1,000 randomly sequenced numbers between 1 and 1,000 were generated. The program output the numbers to a file. The numbers were then pasted from the output file into the word data file. Again this was time saving as generating random numbers for such a large data set is very time consuming if done manually.

Each subject thus had a unique identifier. By mail merging this identifier to the survey form it was possible to prevent sending reminders to those who had already responded. After the first round, 497 responses were received. Had these responses not been tracked reminders would have had to be sent to everyone. This would undoubtedly be annoying for those who had replied but would also have cost nearly another £100 in postage.

Data tracking As surveys were returned they were categorised and entered into a 'Replied' field within the data file. Thus if the 'Replied' field was still blank no reply had been received: '0' indicated a blank reply, '1' a useable reply, '2' replies from non-nurse teachers (Not NT) and '3' replies in which the question about gender was not answered. This was a useful exercise as it allowed selective reminders to be sent to those subjects where the 'Replied' field was still blank. It also gave some analysis but this was limited. Word 97 can perform some maths functions, but for such a large data set better results were found using the spreadsheet Excel 97. It was very easy to move the data from Word 97 to Excel 97. A simple copy/paste was carried out. As Excel 97 is part of the Office 97 suite, it was also easy to make the existing Word 97 merge files look for the data source in the Excel 97. For researchers wishing to do such analysis it makes sense to create the data file in Excel 97 from the outset. Table 1 shows the sort of analysis that can be achieved.

Email and the Web Subjects were offered the choice of returning the

Table 1. Analysis of returns showing percentages by institution.					
Institution	No reply	Blank 0	Usable 1	Not NT 2	No gender 3	Total returns
1	32%	2%	61%	5%	0%	68%
2	19%	2%	64%	13%	2%	81%
3	6%	6%	85%	3%	0%	94%
4	20%	0%	70%	9%	1%	80%
5	39%	0%	44%	17%	0%	61%
6	12%	4%	74%	8%	2%	88%
7	11%	7%	77%	2%	3%	89%
8	13%	5%	78%	5%	0%	87%

survey via the paper-based copy that was sent to them or via the Web. Initially a standard Web-based form was written which enabled data to be input and submitted by email. The resulting output format from this however was found to be inadequate. Items were concatenated together in the resulting email making it difficult to read. Another solution had to be found. A Common Gateway

Issues in research

Interface (CGI) script was needed to change the output from the form into a more readable format. None of the authors at that time had any working knowledge of writing such scripts.

To find a solution the authors sent an email to a discussion list for staff interested in developing Web-based resources. Within a week a number of replies were received and a solution was found. The authors were pointed to a site on the Web. Wright (4) provides a site that offers free CGI scripts. One such script, FormMail, provided the solution needed. The CGI script allows the output to be configured in a number of ways. For this survey these included:

● Stipulating a subject line for the email output to enable web surveys to be easily recognised amongst the other email

● Setting certain form items to be compulsory, for example, ID number

● Sorting the form items into any order required, each item is returned on its own line greatly enhancing readability

● Setting a URL to show when the form has been submitted, for example, a 'Thank you' page.

In total 548 useable replies were received. Disappointingly, only 34 (6.2 per cent) were received via the Web form. The authors feel certain however, that as technological communication becomes more common place, the Web will develop into a very useful tool for nurse researchers.

Conclusion

If computers were not available to the authors this study would probably still have been carried out, but on a smaller scale. A postal survey on this scale would not have been considered without the aid of a computer. It is hoped that this paper readily demonstrates how the nurse researcher can utilise the power of the computer to their advantage.

Carol Cooper CertEd, BEd, RGN, RNT, CertOET, CompBCS, is C&IT Development Manager, School of Nursing, Midwifery and Health Visiting, University of Manchester. Jackie Oldham PhD, BSc(Hons),

RGN, is Director, Centre for Rehabilitation Science, University of Manchester, Manchester Royal Infirmary and Consultant Editor, Nurse Researcher, Nurse Researcher. Val Hillier BSc(Hons Maths), PhD, MSc (Statistics), is Senior Lecturer, Department of Medical Biophysics, University of Manchester.

References.
1. English National Board for Nursing Midwifery and Health Visiting. *Teacher Establishment Data Synopsis.* London, ENB. 1996.
2. English National Board for Nursing Midwifery and Health Visiting. *Applicant Handbook.* London, ENB. 1996.
3. Cooper CD. Survey – *Does gender affect Nurse Teachers' attitudes to Information Technology (IT)?* Web page. Available at http://www.man.ac.uk/~mdplscc/research/ (Accessed 20 April 1998).
4. Wright M. *Matt's Script Archive.* Web page. 1997. Available at http://www.worldwidemart.com/scripts/ (Accessed 27 April 1998).

Issues in research

Research round-up

A regular look at forthcoming events, courses and information relevant to nursing research.

Appointments

Professor Lorraine Smith is the new chair of the RCN Research Society (Scotland). She can be contacted at the School of Nursing, Midwifery and Health Visiting, University of Glasgow, 68 Oakfield Avenue, Glasgow G12 8LS. Tel: 0141 330 4051. E-mail: L.N.Smith@clinmed.gla.ac.uk. **Andrew Elliot** is confirmed as secretary to the committee. He can be contacted at the Diabetes Centre, Ward 34, Western General Hospital, Crewe Road, Edinburgh EH4 2XU. Tel: 0131 537 1752. **Susan Kerr** is the group's treasurer and is available at the School of Nursing and Midwifery, University of Glasgow. E-mail: sk33p@clinmed.gla.ac.uk

Conferences

The Faculty of Nursing, Royal College of Surgeons in Ireland are holding the 18th Annual Nursing Research conference on February 24-25, 1999, with the opening address on the evening of Wednesday 24. The theme of the conference is **'Research Utilization – A Challenge for Nurses in the Millennium'**. Further information is available from Faculty of Nursing, Royal College of Surgeons in Ireland, 123 St Stephen's Green, Dublin 2. Tel: +353 1 402 2202/402 2206. Fax: +353 1 402 2465. E-mail: +facnursing@rcsi.ie

The 4th European Mental Health Nursing Conference, **'Valuing Mental Health Nursing'**, takes place in Jersey, the Channel Islands, on February 19-21, 1999. Further information is available from Anna-Maria Nilsson, Conference Organiser, Royal College of Nursing, 20 Cavendish Square, London W1M 0AB.